D. H. LAWRENCE
and his world

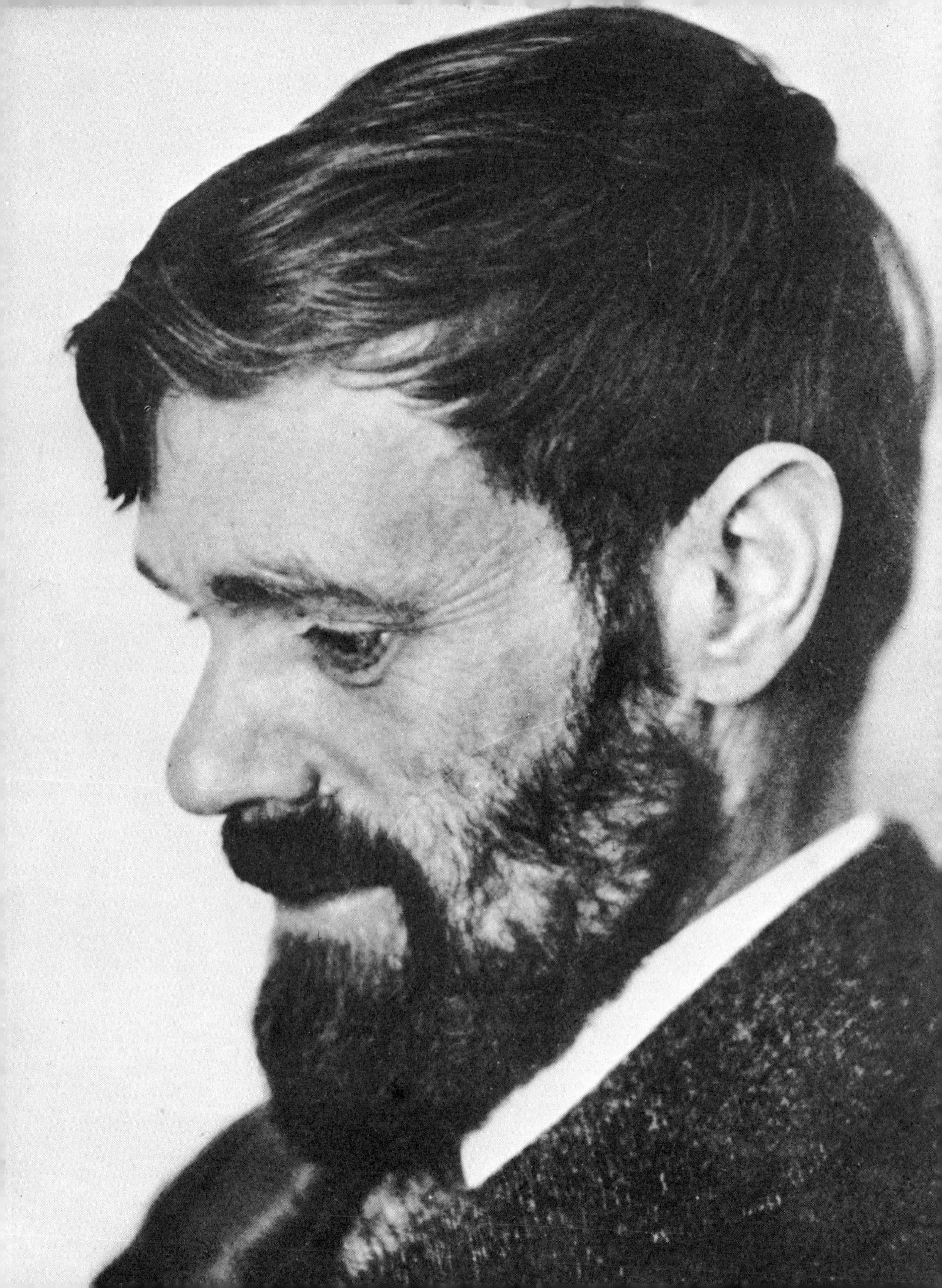

D. H. LAWRENCE
and his world

BY HARRY T. MOORE AND WARREN ROBERTS

A STUDIO BOOK

THE VIKING PRESS · NEW YORK

Copyright 1966 Harry T. Moore and Warren Roberts & Thames and Hudson Ltd in all countries of the International Copyright Union. All rights reserved.

Published in 1966 by The Viking Press, Inc. 625 Madison Avenue, New York, N.Y. 10022

Library of Congress catalog card number: 65-15109

Printed in Great Britain by Dawson Rossiter Ltd.

Brinsley colliery. 'Look how it heaps together, like something alive almost—a big creature that you don't know.' *(Sons and Lovers)*

D. H. LAWRENCE, whose full name was David Herbert Richards Lawrence, was born on 11 September 1885 in Eastwood, a hill town in the Nottinghamshire coalfield. His birthplace was a small brick house in Victoria Street, which slanted down towards the colliery area, north of the town, where his father went to work early each morning, to spend his day digging in the pits. The front room of the ground floor of the house had for a while been a shop where Mrs Lawrence had sold linen and the lace for which her native Nottingham, a few miles away, was famous.

Family

Lawrence's 'come-from', as background or ancestry is called in that part of the Midlands, has a special interest. He had two forceful grandfathers. On the paternal side there was John Lawrence, a Nottingham man who had gone to the Eastwood region in the 1850s to be company tailor at the Brinsley colliery. In his youth he had been an outstanding rower and boxer. His grandson always remembered his early glimpses of the tailor shop with its huge rolls of flannel from which the miners' workclothes were made.

The other grandfather, George Beardsall, also from Nottingham, was a quite different kind of man. He was an engineer who for a long time had been employed at Sheerness. His family, originally tanners from Derbyshire, had

Lawrence's birthplace: 8a Victoria Street. '... nasty, red-brick, flat-faced dwellings with dark slate roofs.' (*Nottingham and the Mining Countryside*)

(*Centre*) Long Row, Nottingham. 'Shops down the Long Row were deep in obscurity, and the shadow was full of colour.' (*Sons and Lovers*)

(*Below*) Nottingham Road, Eastwood. 'The car ploughed uphill through the long squalid straggle ... the blackened brick dwellings, the black slate roofs glistening their sharp edges, the mud black with coal-dust, the pavements wet and black.' (*Lady Chatterley's Lover*)

The Lawrence family. Standing: Emily Una, George, William. Seated: Lettice Ada, Mrs Lydia Lawrence, David Herbert Lawrence, Arthur John Lawrence

done well in Nottingham but had lost their money during various financial disasters in the lace industry in the nineteenth century, and George Beardsall was a man of some bitterness. He was also fervently religious, and often preached in the Methodist chapels. His family was related by marriage to the Lawrences, and it was at the house of a relative that D. H. Lawrence's mother, Lydia Beardsall, met her future husband, Arthur John Lawrence.

They were married at Christmastime in 1875, when Arthur Lawrence was twenty-nine years old and his wife six years younger. She had been a school-teacher, and she was, as her son once wrote, 'a superior soul'. One of her sisters, Lettice, made a distinguished marriage to Fritz Krenkow, a German scholar of oriental languages who became a lecturer at Cambridge University. Lydia's grandfather on her mother's side, John Newton, had worked in the lace factories as a 'twisthand', but he was also a noted hymn writer: *Sovereignty* is still sung in the Nonconformist chapels. D. H. Lawrence, who was brought

Albert Street Congregational Chapel, Eastwood. 'The Congregational chapel, which thought itself superior, was built of rusticated sandstone and had a steeple, but not a very high one.' (*Lady Chatterley's Lover*)

(*Right*) Lawrence (third row down, second from the left) with some of his classmates at Beauvale Board School. 'I was a delicate pale brat with a snuffy nose, whom most people treated quite gently as just an ordinary delicate little lad. (*Autobiographical Sketch*)

(*Far right*) Beauvale Board School, Eastwood

Early life

up in his father's Congregationalist faith, has in his essay *Hymns in a Man's Life* told of the influence, upon his vision and writing, of the songs bellowed out in the miners' bethel. When Lawrence was a young man he left Congregationalism, took up Unitarianism for a while, then gradually developed his own religion of 'blood knowledge' and mysterious 'dark gods'.

Lawrence had two brothers and two sisters, and was the next-to-youngest in the family. He was from the first a frail child, with brownish hair that turned red as he grew up. He was never very athletic, and often played with the girls of his age. His mother encouraged him in his studies at Beauvale Board School, where one of his older brothers, William Ernest, had had a good record before becoming a successful young businessman in London. Lawrence, who disliked his first name, David, was always known as Bert to his family. At twelve he won a county council scholarship to Nottingham High School, and for three years took the train daily to travel the eight miles into the town.

Nottingham High School. 'When I was twelve I got a county council scholarship, twelve pounds a year, and went to Nottingham High School.' *(Autobiographical Sketch)*

His earlier childhood had been a mixture of joy and misery. He was happy when he could walk through the country about Eastwood, of which he was later to write so intimately. Sometimes he and his sisters visited their grandparents at Brinsley, north of Eastwood, walking over the fields amid the creaking headstocks and the black chimneysmoke of the collieries. Farmland surrounded the mines, and great trees stood here and there in clumps. There are many memorials of the past. Annesley Park, Newstead Abbey, and Hucknall Torkard are all associated with Byron. Close to Eastwood, the ruins of a fourteenth-century castle stand up jaggedly at Greasley. The shattered Beauvale Abbey provided the background for Lawrence's medieval story *A Fragment of Stained Glass*. He also frequently drew upon High Park Wood, in which the Abbey stands; Moorgreen Reservoir, next to the wood; and the nearby manor-house, Lamb Close, home of the Barbers, who for centuries had owned the Eastwood collieries. Lamb Close figures prominently in Lawrence's first novel *The White Peacock* (1911), in *Women in Love* (1920) and *Lady Chatterley's Lover* (1928).

Moorgreen colliery. '... the coal-mine lifted its great mounds and its patterned head-stocks, the black railway with the trucks at rest looked like a harbour just below, a large bay of railroad with anchored wagons.' (*Women in Love*)

Felley Mill (below right), Underwood Church (far right), Haggs Farm (far left). 'That's the country of my heart. From the hills, if you look across at Underwood wood, you'll see a tiny red farm on the edge of the wood. That was Miriam's farm—where I got my first incentive to write.' (Letter)

The country always seemed wonderful to the boy, when he could get out of sight of the mines. The colliers came home at dusk, their faces masked with coal-dust, singing as they walked along the streets. When they were home, they stripped off their upper clothing, and their wives washed the dust from their backs. This process seemed to fascinate and horrify the young Lawrence, who was later to describe it in several stories and to put it on the stage in his play *The Widowing of Mrs Holroyd* (1914).

Parents

Lawrence's unhappiness as a child was caused by the fierce quarrels between his parents amid their grinding poverty. His father was a robust, black-bearded little man who sometimes stopped at the pub on the way home and spent part of his wages, on which the family lived, drinking with his friends. This infuriated his wife, who was of the temperance persuasion. She would nag him,

(Left) British School, Albert Street, Eastwood
(Right) The Breach, Eastwood. The Lawrence family lived in this house from 1887 to 1891. 'We lived in the Breach, in a corner house. A field-path came down under a great hawthorn hedge.' *(Nottingham and the Mining Countryside)*

and he would shout back, sometimes striking her; once, when she was pregnant, he pushed her out of the house and locked her out for the night. Lawrence described these lacerating quarrels in his work, particularly in his novel *Sons and Lovers* (1913), of which he said that the first half, the childhood part, was based on real events. The children took their mother's side when they were small; Lawrence later said that he felt he had been wrong in this because he had failed to realize his father's worth as man intensely alive, with a relish for living. Even as late as the time of writing *Sons and Lovers* Lawrence was mostly on the mother's side, though in that book the portrait of the father is partly sympathetic.

Lawrence always bore many spiritual scars from those savage fights between his parents. His mother battled, and successfully, to keep her sons out of the mine and her daughters out of domestic service. But it was at terrible cost. The mines themselves were always in Lawrence's consciousness, perhaps providing the symbol of darkness he used so often in his work. In later life he wrote that the colliers 'brought with them above ground the curious intimacy of the mine, the naked sort of contact, and if I think of my childhood it is always as if there

Moorgreen Reservoir. 'The lake was blue and fair, the meadows sloped down in sunshine on one side, the thick dark woods dropped steeply on the other.'
(*Women in Love*)

was a lustrous sort of inner darkness like the gloss of coal in which we moved and had our being.'

Mrs Lawrence, disappointed in her marriage, turned her strong love upon her sons, first upon Ernest, who was the brightest and most promising. But in the autumn of 1901 he died at twenty-three, in London, of pneumonia combined with erysipelas. For a long time after the funeral his mother was dazed and half alive. Then her son Bert became ill, and she turned her fierce love on him as she nursed him through an attack of pneumonia. He had finished high school and had continued to go into Nottingham daily, working as a clerk in an artificial-limbs factory. After his illness he did not return to that employment: he had a slow convalescence and then became a teacher of other colliers' sons at the British School in Eastwood.

During these years, the Lawrence family had moved several times. In Lawrence's infancy they went to live in the miners' quarters at the bottom of the hill to the north of Eastwood, a place called the Breach (the Bottoms of *Sons and Lovers*). It was a dismal area, soot-soaked, though it was at the edge of open country; and Mrs Lawrence disliked it. But because she considered herself above the other colliers' wives she was glad to have an end house where she could keep up a garden. At the beginning of the nineties, the Lawrences moved to the hill above the Breach, to a house in Walker Street from which they could look out on the sloping farmlands, the smoking mines, and the patches of Sherwood Forest: 'I lived in that house from the age of 6 to 18, and know that view better than any in the world.'

Jessie Chambers

In that landscape there was a small farm just north of Moorgreen Reservoir and Lamb Close House: the Haggs farm at Willey Spring, where the Chambers family lived. Lawrence had met them just before his illness at sixteen. He became a fast friend of one of the boys, Alan, and established one of the most

Lamb Close House, Moorgreen. 'It was a long, low old house, a sort of manor farm, that spread along the top of a slope just beyond the narrow little lake . . . .' *(Women in Love)*

The Misk Hills and the road to Haggs Farm. 'To me it seemed . . . an extremely beautiful countryside, just between the red sandstone and the oak-trees of Nottingham, and the cold limestone, the ash-trees, the stone fences of Derbyshire.' *(Nottingham and the Mining Countryside)*

important relationships of his life with Alan's sister, Jessie, who was to be the Miriam of *Sons and Lovers*. A year younger than Lawrence, this farm girl was a dreamer, and she became obsessed with the slim youth who so often walked out across the fields to the Haggs or pedalled there along the roads on his bicycle. Jessie and Lawrence began to read together, sitting in the fields or under the trees in the forest. They read aloud many of the great English novels and poems. George Eliot meant much to them because she had written of Derbyshire, only a few miles away; even Jane Austen had set some scenes in her fiction there. Such books as *Lorna Doone* particularly moved the young couple, and they named the adjoining woodlands Bagley Forest. Later, when Lawrence learned French, he and Jessie read Paul Verlaine. They obtained their books from the library of the Mechanics' Institute at Eastwood or read serials in various journals. And they studied together in the farm kitchen of the Haggs.

Haggs Farm, Underwood. 'The farm and buildings, three sides of a quadrangle, embraced the sunshine towards the wood.' *(Sons and Lovers)*

Lawrence sometimes helped Jessie's father and brothers in mowing hay. As Mr Chambers said, 'Work goes like fun when Bert's here.' Lawrence was lively, imaginative, playful, and for years the Haggs was his second home. His mother disapproved of these friends, particularly of Jessie, in whom she saw a rival. The conflict between Mrs Lawrence and Jessie provided Lawrence with one of the principal themes of *Sons and Lovers*. In the book, as in life, the girl eventually lost because the boy was too closely bound to his mother. But Lawrence's relationship with Jessie lasted nearly a dozen years. Jessie was by then in her middle twenties, and she wanted to make the attachment permanent. But Lawrence was still incapable of this because of his mother's influence. He had a love affair with an older woman, Alice Dax, who was married, a relationship on which that between Paul Morel and Clara Dawes in *Sons and Lovers* was partly based; but this too came to nothing.

Jessie Chambers. 'Her beauty—that of a shy, wild, quiveringly sensitive thing—seemed nothing to her. Even her soul, so strong for rhapsody, was not enough. She must have something to reinforce her pride. . . .' *(Sons and Lovers)*

When Mrs Lawrence died of cancer in December 1910, her son was unable to shake himself free from his emotional ties with her and went through what he called his 'sick year'. It was not until 1912, when he met his future wife, that he found himself able to consider a permanent attachment.

Meanwhile, after teaching for a year at Eastwood, he was reassigned, as a pupil-teacher, to the school in the nearby borough of Ilkeston, in Derbyshire. A number of Lawrence's friends were also pupil-teachers there; usually they took the morning train over from Eastwood, and in the afternoon walked back across the fields. Except for the rather solemn Jessie Chambers, who liked to have Lawrence to herself, they were a merry group, calling themselves the Pagans. At this time Lawrence was extremely interested in Louise Burrows, a girl from a town near Ilkeston-Cossall, the Cossethay of his novel *The Rainbow* (1915), in which he drew upon Louise Burrows for part of the portrait of the heroine, Ursula Brangwen.

Lawrence attended the pupil-teacher centre from 1903 to 1905. Early in the morning the apprentice teachers received instruction from older members of the

Pupil-teacher

University College, Nottingham, which Lawrence attended from 1906 to 1908. 'Its rather pretty, plaything, Gothic form was almost a style, in the dirty industrial town.' *(The Rainbow)*

staff; then, when the school opened for the regular business of the day, the young people taught the children's classes. Lawrence spoke later of the 'savage teaching of collier lads', and in describing Ursula's experiences in *The Rainbow* he showed how rough the boys could be. But in December 1904, new horizons began to gleam brightly before Lawrence: in the King's Scholarship Examination, he came out first in all England and Wales. He received a scholarship grant to what was then Nottingham University College, though he had to wait a year before entering because he lacked the twenty pounds required for advance fees. He spent that year as an uncertificated teacher at the British School in Eastwood, saving what money he could. And his mother skimped to help him. In September 1906, the month he became twenty-one, he again began taking the daily train to Nottingham, to attend college there.

In those days the institution was not where the present Nottingham University is, along the River Trent southwest of the city; it was in the mock-Gothic building in Shakespeare Street which is now the local library. Lawrence did

Lawrence on his twenty-first birthday. '... clean-shaven, bright young prig in a high collar like a curate, guaranteed to counteract all the dark and sinister effect of all the newspaper photographs.' (Letter)

not read for a degree, but took the two-year course for the teacher's certificate. He was disappointed with his studies, and later said that his two years at the University College 'had meant mere disillusionment instead of the contact of living men.' But he worked hard and was particularly interested in botany and in the French course taught by Professor Ernest Weekley.

Lawrence and Jessie still went for long walks and read books together. The Lawrence family had moved from the Walker Street house in 1902 to what is now 97 Lynn Croft, the last family home they were to have. Lawrence had begun painting, chiefly copying such then popular artists as Maurice Greiffenhagen and Frank Brangwyn. At seventeen he had started to write poetry, later taking up fiction as well. He spent about four years on his first novel, *The White Peacock*.

School-master

In the autumn of 1908, Lawrence went to teach at Croydon, south of London, at the fairly new Davidson Road School, at a salary of ninety pounds a year. He remained there for about three and a half years, until ill health forced him to retire in the winter of 1911/12. He was a highly successful teacher at Croydon, where his eager imagination caught the enthusiasm of his students. It is strange that Lawrence, who in his later work consistently attacked science, should in his youth have taught it as ardently as he taught literature. Towards the end of his life he was to write: ' "Knowledge" has killed the sun, making it a ball of gas, with spots; "knowledge" has killed the moon—it is a dead little earth fretted with extinct craters as with smallpox; the machine has killed the earth for us . . . The two ways of knowing, for man, are knowing in terms of apartness, which is mental, rational, scientific, and knowing in terms of togetherness, which is religious and poetic.'

Helen Corke

While at Croydon, Lawrence frequently went home to Eastwood. Away from his mother's influence, he became engaged to a fellow-teacher at Croydon, Agnes Holt. But he was soon far more interested in a girl who was an instructor in another school in the area, Helen Corke. He virtually brought her back to

Davidson Road School, Croydon, where Lawrence taught 1908/11. 'A red rock, silent and shadowless, clung round with clusters of shouting lads.' *(School on the Outskirts)*
(Right) Helen Corke *c.* 1912

Felley Mill pond. 'The whole place was gathered in the musing of old age. The thick-piled trees on the far shore were too dark and sober to dally with the sun; the weeds stood crowded and motionless... The water lay softly, intensely still.' (*The White Peacock*)

life after she had been through a shattering experience: she had run off to the Isle of Wight with her violin teacher, a well-known musician, H. B. MacCartney of the Carl Rosa opera company, who was a married man. In spite of the idyllic surroundings—a moonlit summer coast—the relationship turned out to be an unhappy one. After MacCartney returned home, he killed himself. His suicide created a sensation. Helen Corke was in a state of shock when Lawrence met her soon afterwards, in the autumn of 1909; he told her about the spirit of tragedy, took her to see performances of tragedies in London, and accompanied her on long walks across the North Downs. She described her experiences in poetry (*Songs of Autumn*, 1956) and in a prose version which was included in her novel *Neutral Ground* (1933). Lawrence with her permission based his second novel, *The Trespasser* (1912), upon her prose account of the MacCartney affair.

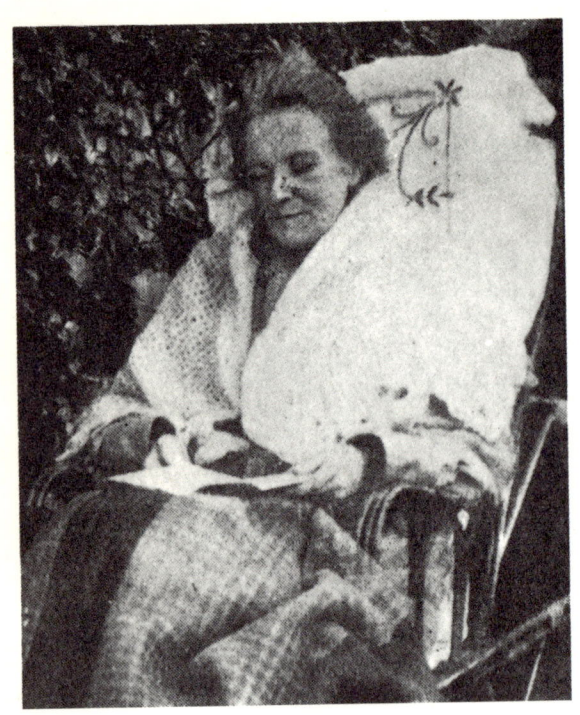

Lawrence's mother at the time of her last illness. '... they used to carry her downstairs, sometimes even into the garden.... And she watched the tangled sunflowers dying, the chrysanthemums coming out, and the dahlias.' (*Sons and Lovers*)

Edward Garnett *c.* 1911. 'He [Hueffer] introduced me to Edward Garnett, who, somehow, introduced me to the world.' (Preface to *Collected Poems*)

Edward Garnett

Meanwhile, in December 1910, his mother died. The poems he wrote immediately after this show how intensely the event affected him. He could not enjoy the appearance of *The White Peacock* in January 1911 because his mother had been too ill to read or even appreciate the significance of the advance copy he put in her hands.

He had made his professional debut as a writer in the November 1909 issue of the *English Review,* with some poems Jessie Chambers had sent its editor, Ford Madox Ford (then Ford Madox Hueffer). Lawrence became known in London literary circles and met H. G. Wells, Ezra Pound, and other authors. It was Hueffer's friend, the writer Violet Hunt, who took the manuscript of *The White Peacock* to the firm of Heinemann, which published it. But *The Trespasser* went to the house of Gerald Duckworth, whose reader was Edward Garnett, the discoverer of W. H. Hudson and Charles Montague Doughty, and the friend of Joseph Conrad. Garnett encouraged the young Lawrence and was his friend and mentor for several years.

Felley Mill pond. '... the wood sweeps down and stands with its feet washed round with waters. We broke our way along the shore, crushing the sharp-scented wild mint, whose odour checks the breath, and examining here and there among the marshy places ragged nests of water-fowl, now deserted.' *(The White Peacock)*

The White Peacock had been a mild critical success. Lawrence in this book wrote idyllically of the Eastwood area, not describing the mines and the lives of the colliers, but placing the story in a farm and country-house setting. The young narrator, Cyril Beardsall, has a Lawrence-like sensitivity but comes from a more refined background: his mother lives in a lodge in a wooded park. His sister Lettie, the proud peacock of the title, is in love with a youthful farmer named George Saxton, but she passes him over to marry the young squire of the region, Leslie Tempest. George loves Lettie and also feels an affection for Cyril that reaches its high point in the chapter 'A Poem of Friendship', in which the physical contact of the two young men, in an episode that seems more athletic than erotic, foreshadows a somewhat similar scene in Lawrence's fifth novel, *Women in Love*.

'*The White Peacock*'

The Misk Hills

Having failed with Lettie, George marries his cousin Meg. Cyril, returning to the area on several visits after he has left it, watches George deteriorate into drunkenness and a general stupefaction. If Lawrence had placed the fictional equivalents of his family in a superior environment to the one they knew in life —in this book the father is a shabby outcast who dies in a distant place—he at least drew on experience in describing heavy drinking, which he had observed in his father and now transferred to the character of George.

There is much literary chatter in *The White Peacock*: the young intellectuals speak in bookish terms. The language of the narrative is also too literary at times,

Felley Mill Farm. '... at the bottom, where the end of the farm buildings rose high and grey, there was a plumtree which had been crucified to the wall, and which had broken away and leaned forward from bondage. Now under the boughs were hidden great mist-bloomed, crimson treasures, splendid globes.' *(The White Peacock)*

though it is always lucid. It has little of the force that Lawrence was later to develop; only an occasional passage heralds a promising future, such as the section beginning 'I was born in September, and love it best of all the months.' Edward Garnett, however, knew how to recognize a writer who would endure; to him Lawrence seemed a man of brilliant prospects on the strength of his early stories and poems and *The White Peacock*.

In the spring of 1912, after Lawrence had given up teaching at Croydon and had returned to the Midlands, he wondered whether he might not try for a teaching position at a German university. To enquire about this he went into

The Weekleys

Nottingham to see his former French teacher at the University College, Professor Ernest Weekley, and at his home met Mrs Weekley. She was German, the daughter of Baron Friedrich von Richthofen, a government official at Metz. The mother of three children, Frieda was restless in her marriage to a linguist fourteen years older than she was, whom she considered dull. Frieda at thirty-two was vivacious and life-hungry; she was having extra-marital love affairs in Nottingham. When Lawrence, a twenty-six-year-old poet with a red moustache, appeared, she was attracted to him and he to her. She tried to draw him into the orbit of her love affairs, but Lawrence refused to play her game: he wanted to attempt a durable union.

In London, he had not managed to create such a relationship with Helen Corke. And Agnes Holt had married someone else. Lawrence's love affair with the married woman in Eastwood had dissolved. He had apparently become engaged, in a half-hearted way, to Louise Burrows, but this relationship failed to last. He had kept in touch with Jessie Chambers, who had apparently expected to marry him; but for all their mutual sympathy he found her too possessive. It was the very qualities she had in common with his mother that drove him away from her, though throughout his life he was fatally drawn into friendships with will-motored women. Jessie, who never again spoke or wrote to Lawrence after reading the proofsheets of *Sons and Lovers*, a book for

Cowley (now Hillcrest), Victoria Crescent, Mapperley, once the home of Professor Ernest Weekley. Lawrence and Frieda met here in April 1912

Frieda Weekley (born von Richthofen). 'She is the daughter of Baron von Richthofen... but she's splendid, she is really.' (Letter)

which she had provided some notes and important narrative passages, was deeply hurt by the portrait of Miriam, which Lawrence had drawn with the necessarily cruel detachment of the artist. As for Frieda, she was strong-willed in her way, but her will did not coldly dictate to her emotions. She had an élan which lighted up the beauty she had when young, she had almost savage affections, and she showed from the first a deep understanding of the artist and his problems. She was far from a perfect mate—she could be treacherous in love and was to prove capable of betraying Lawrence as well as being often quarrelsome; yet her relationship with him during the remaining eighteen years of his life was a great and important one. Her influence on his work was profound.

(Top) Frieda with Ernest Weekley and his parents
(Centre) Frieda (right) with her son, Montague, in 1901
(Left) Frieda and Ernest Weekley in Germany

Baroness von Richthofen, Frieda's mother

Baron Friedrich von Richthofen, Frieda's father, in 1872

Germany

Lawrence and Frieda left for Metz on 3 May 1912. Frieda had not broken completely with her husband; she was ostensibly going to attend the jubilee celebrating the fiftieth anniversary of her father's entrance into the army. Lawrence stayed quietly at a hotel in Metz, where Frieda secretly introduced him to her two sisters. Later, when Frieda and Lawrence, in one of their clandestine meetings, were walking about the fortifications in Metz, the German authorities arrested him as an English spy. Frieda had to ask her father to use his influence to get her lover released, so Lawrence met the shocked elder von Richthofens. He went alone to Waldbröl in the Rhineland to stay with some of his Aunt Lettice's relatives, but constantly wrote Frieda love letters. One of these was from Hennef, where he was 'sitting like a sad swain beside a nice, twittering little river, waiting for the twilight to drop, and my last train to come ... Now for the first time during today, my detachment leaves me, and I know I only love you. The rest is nothing at all. And the promise of life with you is all richness. Now I know.'

These sentiments were repeated in the poem 'Bei Hennef' which was included in *Love Poems*, published in 1913, and also later in *Collected Poems*:

The River Sieg at Hennef, Germany

> *The little river twittering in the twilight,*
> *The wan, wondering look of the pale sky,*
> *This is almost bliss.*

And then, exactly echoing his letter to Frieda, Lawrence ended the poem:

> *You are the call and I am the answer,*
> *You are the wish and I the fulfilment,*
> *You are the night, and I the day.*
>
> *What else ? it is perfect enough.*
> *It is perfectly complete,*
> *You and I,*
> *What more — ?*
> *Strange, how we suffer in spite of this!*

The lonely Lawrence flirted with one of his relatives, Frau Hannah Krenkow, a lively little Rhineland housewife. But within a fortnight Frieda had joined Lawrence at Beuerberg in Bavaria: 'The river is green glacier water. Bavarian villages are white and gay, the churches are baroque, with minarets, white with black caps. Every day it was perfect. There are masses and masses of Alpine flowers, globe flowers, primulas, lilies, orchids—make you dance . . . The lovely brooks we have paddled in, the lovely things we have done!'

The house at Icking, near Munich, where Lawrence and Frieda stayed in 1912. '... there's a balcony, where we sit out, and have meals, and I write. Down below, is the road where the bullock wagons go slowly. Across the road the peasant women work in the wheat. Then the pale, milk-green river runs between the woods and the plain....'
(Letter)

They settled at Icking, below Munich, in the peak-roofed house of a friend of one of Frieda's sisters, and lived on the upper floor which had a balcony that looked out on the Isar. They were happy, but Frieda at times missed her children. The ecstasy of affection and conflict between the two lovers appears in Lawrence's series of poems *Look! We Have Come Through!* (1917), which he began writing then and finished five years later.

While Lawrence and Frieda were at Icking, Garnett's young son David came to see them. He has described Lawrence as he appeared at that time: his broad though not high forehead, short lumpy nose, scrubby red moustache, and rounded, Philip IV-like chin. Frieda looked sturdy and noble: 'Her eyes were green, with a lot of tawny yellow in them, the nose straight ... she was extraordinarily like a lioness.' Garnett discovered that Lawrence could sit writing while people moved about the room and talked; when he put his pen down, he would often show his talents as a mimic. Garnett's picture of the time is one illuminated by delight. He always remained Frieda's friend, though in another three years he had done with Lawrence, who tried to interfere too much in his life. But in 1928 he wrote a generous letter to Lawrence, praising him for *Lady Chatterley's Lover*.

David Garnett

Lawrence *c.* 1912

Early work   During Lawrence's residence at Icking, *The Trespasser* came out, telling the story of Helen Corke's experiences with the musician, H. B. MacCartney. Lawrence's second novel is his poorest, though there are some fine descriptions of the Isle of Wight, to which the music teacher and his girl-student had gone. There is, however, a good deal of fervid imitation—Wagnerian symbolism in this part of the book and, as in *The White Peacock,* the conversation is strained and unreal. At Icking, Lawrence was not amused at the heading which his home-county newspaper, the *Nottinghamshire Guardian,* gave to its review of the novel—'A Reprehensible Jaunt'—but Frieda, who was enjoying her own reprehensible jaunt, chuckled over the caption.

Lago di Garda, Italy. 'The water of the lake is of the most beautiful dark blue colour you can imagine—purple in the shade, and emerald green where it washes over the white rocks.' (Letter)

In August, Lawrence and Frieda began walking across the Tyrolese Alps. David Garnett and his friend Harold Hobson joined them for part of the trip. Lawrence's destination was Lago di Garda, associated with the Roman poet, Catullus; the upper part of this lake was then in Austrian possession. Lawrence and Frieda settled in Gargnano, a little town on the western shore of the lake, in Italian territory. Lawrence's descriptions of the village life—of the little *trattoria*, the theatre, the dark interior of the church, 'the spinner and the monks', and various other features of the place—appear in articles he sent to journals at the time, later collected in his *Twilight in Italy* (1916). It was at Gargnano in November 1912 that Lawrence completed *Sons and Lovers,* on which he had been working for several years.

Meanwhile, what Lawrence in the 'Argument' to the *Look! We Have Come Through!* poems spoke of as 'the conflict of love and hate . . . between the man and the woman' went on. The tenderness between the lovers was violated when

Lawrence and Frieda

(Below) Villa Igéa, Gargnano.
'Gargnano is a tumbledown Italian place straggling along the lake. It is only accessible by steamer, because of the rocky mountains at the back. The Villa Igéa is just across the road from the lake, and looks on the water.' (Letter)

(Above) San Tommaso, Gargnano.
'It always remains to me that San Tommaso and its terrace hang suspended above the village, like the lowest step of heaven, of Jacob's ladder.'
(Twilight in Italy)

the post came from England, bringing mention or reminders of Frieda's children. When she moaned over them, Lawrence would often comment snappily, and another battle would start. Lawrence was having his own agonies in sloughing off his past while writing—a healing and cleansing experience—of the struggles of Paul Morel in *Sons and Lovers*. Frieda once handed Lawrence what she called a skit, 'Paul Morel, or His Mother's Darling', of which Lawrence icily said, 'This kind of thing isn't called a skit.' It was possibly at this time (although it could have been earlier, in Bavaria) that Frieda wrote her marginal comments on the exercise-book manuscript of one of Lawrence's poems to his mother: 'I hate it—Good God!!!! I hate it!' At greater length she added (and this has not been published before):

David Garnett by D. H. Lawrence. 'By Jove, I reckon his parents have done joyously well for that young man.' (Letter)

Yes, worse luck! What a poem to write! Yes, you are free, poor devil, from the heart's home life free, lonely you shall be, you have chosen it, you chose it freely! Now go your way—Misery, a sad old woman's misery you have chosen, you poor man, and you cling to it with all your power. I have tried, I have fought, I have nearly killed myself in the battle to get you in connection with myself and other people, early I proved to myself that I can love, but never you—Now I will leave you for some days and I will see if being alone will help you to see me as I am, I will heal again by myself, you cannot help me, you are a sad thing. I know your secret and your despair, I have seen you ashamed—I love you better, that is my reward.

Yet their relationship went on, through quarrels and dismay and poverty. Writing *Sons and Lovers* helped Lawrence, and so did Frieda, who was strong enough eventually to overcome the beyond-the-grave influence of his mother. As she once said of the situation, 'I think a man is born twice: first his mother bears him, then he has to be reborn from the woman he loves.' Of course

David Garnett. 'Don't fall in love for fear you have to scrub floors and fetch groceries.' (Letter)

Lawrence, with his brilliant imagination and reverence for every manifestation of life, made his own contribution to their existence together. He also gave Frieda a tenderness she had never known before: once when she hit her head against a shutter and was somewhat stunned, Lawrence astonished her by his 'agony of sympathy and tenderness'. In the past when she had hurt herself, no one had cared, and now 'to be so enveloped in tenderness was a miracle in itself for me.' Of course they quarreled through the rest of their lives, all through their subsequent marriage; as Frieda said in court after Lawrence's death, when there was a question about his will and estate, 'We fought like hell!' But there were many times of tranquillity, too. Those who wrote memoirs of the Lawrences were apt to remember the few but spectacular moments of violence and forget the long periods of peace and gentleness. Also, as Frieda has noted, most of the quarrels took place when others were present.

Jacket design: possibly by Ernest Collings to whom Lawrence sent proofs of *Sons and Lovers* from Italy. Thus Collings would know of the Carson, Waite & Co. initials on the coal wagons

'Sons and Lovers'

In April 1913 Lawrence and Frieda left Italy and went back to Bavaria by rail. *Sons and Lovers,* published in May, received several good reviews, but the sale was not large, though more encouraging than that of *Love Poems,* which had come out in February.

Sons and Lovers was the first clear indication of Lawrence's stature as a writer: for those with discernment, his third novel placed him among the significant authors of the day, indeed of the entire English tradition. Unlike *The White Peacock,* this book did not idealize the author's childhood and youth, but presented a grim picture of his early life as a collier's son: the heavy-drinking father, the long-suffering mother, the depressing environment ('it was as if dismalness had soaked through and through everything'), the boy's futile attempt to establish an emotional union with the farm girl, his despair at the death of his mother. Ten years later, Lawrence said he wished he had been fairer to his father in this book; yet, however unconsciously, Lawrence showed sympathy with his vigorous and earth-bound father, whom he depicted in a somewhat tender and even friendly and comic way. The most important conflict in the novel, however, is not between the mother and the father, but between the mother and the son, over the girl known in the book as Miriam Leivers (a farm girl, for although she did not spend all parts of every day labouring on a farm, neither did she live in a town). In the story, Mrs Morel dominates her son Paul and brings about the condition summed up by the title of the chapter 'The Defeat of Miriam'. In the chapter entitled 'Passion', Paul tries to find release in a love affair with a married woman, Clara Dawes; but this relationship is also a failure. When Mrs Morel dies, Paul has the urge to follow her 'into the darkness', but resists the call of death and turns 'back towards the glowing, humming town, quickly'—and in Lawrence's use of the word, *quickly* meant fully alive. This ending, this turning towards life, is prepared for throughout the book, in the very character of Paul. Although his mother dominates and destroys his relationship with Miriam, he is a young man of great spiritual strength who will survive and certainly grow beyond Mrs Morel's influence. All through the book—a most important point—Paul is without self-pity. And he has a tremendous urge towards what Lawrence in later life

Castle Gate buildings, Nottingham. 'It was gloomy and old-fashioned, having low dark shops and dark green house doors with brass knockers, yellow-ochred doorsteps projecting on to the pavement...' (*Sons and Lovers*)

Nottingham Castle. '... they saw the Castle on its bluff of brown, green-bushed rock, in a positive miracle of delicate sunshine.' *(Sons and Lovers)*

often spoke of as livingness. Paul's consciousness is a reflection of that, particularly the poetic quality of his consciousness, embodied in the author's language in representing Paul's experience. *Sons and Lovers,* coming after the somewhat latinized poetic prose of Hardy and the somewhat attenuated poetic prose of Meredith, was a poetic book of a different kind—Anglo-Saxon and strong. Its rhythms had begun to take on a distinctive Lawrencean identity, its landscapes vibrated with colour. The language of *Sons and Lovers* was an important musical and pictorial medium for the story it had to tell, one of powerful emotional conflicts. If the book did not immediately establish itself as an English classic, it at least became known, over the years, as Lawrence's great early achievement, and it was eventually recognized as one of the most substantial novels in English.

Katherine Mansfield.
'... so *charming,* so infinitely charming, in her softness and in her fine, exquisite richness of texture and delicacy of line. There was a certain playfulness about
her too, such a piquancy or ironic suggestion, such an untouched reserve.'
(Women in Love)

In late June, a month after the publication of *Sons and Lovers,* Lawrence and Frieda returned to England. Frieda twice saw her children, then staying with their father's parents in Hampstead. She waited for them in the street near their school, and on the first occasion they happily asked her when she was coming back to them. After this they were told not to speak to her, and the next time she saw them, 'little white faces looked at me as if I were an evil ghost.'

During this London visit, Lawrence and Frieda met John Middleton Murry and Katherine Mansfield, likewise living together (an early marriage of Katherine Mansfield's had not yet been ended). Lawrence came to know them through correspondence, as a contributor to their little magazine *Rhythm,* which

Lawrence (left), Katherine Mansfield, Frieda and Murry in Kensington 1915. 'I'm glad you and Katherine are all right . . . . I know you should stick to the love you have each for the other.' (Letter)

had now become *The Blue Review*. Murry, not long out of Oxford, was trying to make his way in the London literary world. He was wide-mouthed, grey-eyed and handsome, and he wagged his head gently as he talked with a shy smile. Murry perhaps became too close to Lawrence to see him clearly, but he had a fine understanding of writers he did not know, and was destined to become one of the most important twentieth-century British critics.

Katherine Mansfield was a New Zealander, not yet known for her neat and vivid short stories; she was a slim girl with dark large eyes, who wore bangs and was ahead of fashion in having bobbed hair. Murry remembered the first meeting with Lawrence and Frieda, when they all went off to lunch, 'straw hats, and sunshine, and gaiety'. Katherine Mansfield on Frieda's behalf went out to see her children in Hampstead, bringing them messages of love from their mother. Of her relationship and Lawrence's with 'the Murrys', Frieda said years later (in her vital memoir, *Not I, But the Wind* . . . .) that she thought 'theirs was the only spontaneous and jolly friendship that we had.' It would later run into many storms.

Katherine Mansfield

41

Broadstairs, Kent. 'We've got a tent in a little bay on the foreshore, and great waves come and pitch one high up, so I feel like Horace, about to smite my cranium on the sky.' (Letter)

Cynthia Charteris   For part of the summer Lawrence and Frieda went to Kingsgate, on the Kentish coast. Edward Marsh, to whose annual *Georgian Poetry* volumes Lawrence had become a contributor, took him and Frieda to nearby Broadstairs to meet a couple who were to be their friends for a number of years: the Herbert Asquiths. 'Beb' Asquith was the son of the Liberal Prime Minister, H. H. Asquith; he had married Cynthia Charteris, who was shortly (because of a death in the family, elevating her father in rank) to become Lady Cynthia. From the attitude Lawrence expressed a number of times, in his letters and his fiction, he undoubtedly fell partly in love with the glowing Cynthia Asquith, though there was never any question of sexual relations between them. But Lawrence made barmecide love to her through his stories *The Ladybird* and *Glad Ghosts,* and when he chose the name of the heroine of his most famous book, he picked one—Constance Chatterley—suggesting Cynthia Charteris. Lawrence in his writings often played with names in this manner.

42

Lady Cynthia Asquith. 'You were awfully nice to us at Kingsgate. But that your Marylands was such a joy, I might have found myself hurrying over the edge of the cliff in my haste to get away from that half-crystallized nowhere of a place, Kingsgate. . . .' (Letter)

Villino Ettore Gambrosier (centre left), Fiascherino, Italy. 'We have got a tiny four-room cottage amongst the vines, on a little rocky bay down here.' (Letter)

In that summer of 1913, Frieda made little progress in her efforts to obtain a divorce. Her husband was firm and bitter. Early in August she and Lawrence returned briefly to Germany en route to Italy. Frieda took the train from Munich, and Lawrence hiked south through Switzerland to Milan, where he arrived in late September. Soon he and Frieda found a little house at Fiascherino, Lerici, on the Gulf of Spezia, where they remained until the beginning of the next June. Lawrence was working on a novel he then called *The Sisters*. He was to complete one part of this as *The Rainbow* in 1915 and another as *Women in Love* in 1916 (first published in 1920).

The composition of *The Sisters* went slowly at Fiascherino, and Frieda still agonized over her children. Lawrence and Frieda were received by the local English colony, whose members thought them a married couple, and occasionally a visitor from England appeared. One of these was a young writer, Ivy Low, who not long afterward became the wife of Maxim Litvinov, later to be Foreign Minister of Soviet Russia.

Catherine Carswell *c.* 1909. 'How exciting your letter is! . . . I only want to know people who have the courage to live.' (Letter)

When Frieda's divorce came through at the end of May, she and Lawrence planned to travel north again. Once more she took the train and visited her family in Germany, while he walked over the Alps and across France with an engineer from the Vickers-Maxim works at Spezia. Frieda and Lawrence were in London before the end of June, and lunched with Edward Marsh and Rupert Brooke. On 13 July Lawrence and Frieda were married at the Register Office in Kensington, the district in which they were then living. At this time they met several new friends who were to be important to them, including Catherine Jackson, soon to become Catherine Carswell, who after Lawrence's death became one of his first biographers (with *The Savage Pilgrimage,* 1932). They also became acquainted with a relative of Ivy Low, the psychoanalyst Dr David Eder. And the American poet Amy Lowell bustled into London and insisted on having some of Lawrence's poetry for her anthology of Imagists. Murry and Katherine Mansfield were a little jealous of these new friends.

Marriage

Viola Meynell. 'Viola Meynell has lent us this rather beautiful cottage.' (Letter)

Anti-war feeling

At the end of July Lawrence went walking in Westmorland with several men, including the Russian-Jewish refugee, S. S. Koteliansky, who was to be his friend over the years. At Barrow-in-Furness, in early August, they learned that the First World War had broken out. Later that month the Lawrences moved to a cottage at Chesham, Buckinghamshire, where they remained until the following January. During a period of illness there, Lawrence grew the beard he was to wear for the rest of his life.

Lawrence, shocked by the war, said that at this time his soul was in a tomb; it was not dead, but like a corpse it had a flat stone over it: 'and nobody existed, because I did not exist myself.' The title story of his volume which came out in November 1914, *The Prussian Officer,* showed that while he was in Germany he had observed some of the brutal mechanization of the military life there, but this man married to a German wife was not deeply anti-German; he felt that Germany was adolescent and had 'the faults of adolescence'.

Shed Hall, Viola Meynell's cottage at Greatham. 'It is at the foot of the Downs.... It is quite comfortable—there is hot water and a bathroom, and two spare bedrooms... it *is* nice here.' (Letter)

Lawrence in these years rarely uttered a pro-British sentiment about the war; like many English intellectuals he believed that it was in every way an outrage. Frieda wrote a letter to Lady Cynthia Asquith, saying that 'Beb' Asquith shouldn't have to go to the front: didn't it mean anything that he was the Prime Minister's son?

Viola Meynell, a young poet who was the daughter of the Catholic writers Wilfrid and Alice Meynell, offered the Lawrences a house in which they lived from late January until the end of July 1915. This was at Greatham, in Sussex, where Wilfrid Meynell had bought a small circle of old cottages and given them to his daughters for homes, in order to create a little family colony. One of the daughters, Madeline, was married to a brother of E. V. Lucas, the popular essayist. Lawrence looked upon Percy Lucas with a somewhat jaundiced eye, seeing him as a loafer who lived off the bounty of his father-in-law and let himself be controlled by women. He drew a portrait of Lucas in an acid little story, *England, My England,* which became the title of a 1922 collection of tales. The story itself first appeared in the *English Review* in October 1915; Lawrence didn't know until afterwards that Percy Lucas, who had volunteered for the army although past his first youth and father of several children, had been killed in France. Lawrence was sorry about the portrait, but told Catherine Carswell he thought that *England, My England* contained an underlying truth.

Greatham

Lady Ottoline Morrell at Garsington Manor. 'She is like an old, tragic queen who knows that her life has been spent in conflict with a kingdom that was not worth her life.' (Letter)

Lawrence (right), Philip Heseltine (Peter Warlock) and Dikrān Kouyoumdjian (the future Michael Arlen) at Garsington c. 1915. 'Heseltine is a bit backboneless . . . Kouyoumdjian seems a bit blatant and pushing.' (Letter)

A portrait of Lawrence reproduced in *T.P.'s and Cassell's Weekly*, 18 July 1925

While at Greatham he met several other important new friends, among them Lady Ottoline Morrell, member of an aristocratic family from the region in which Lawrence grew up, now married to a commoner, Philip Morrell, a Liberal Member of Parliament. Lady Ottoline collected authors and artists at her homes in Bloomsbury and Garsington, Oxfordshire. One of these was Bertrand Russell, whom she brought to Greatham to meet Lawrence. He and Russell agreed that the war was a monstrosity, and for a while a strong sympathy existed between the two men. But Lawrence was working out his anti-intellectual theories about the power of 'blood-knowledge', and such ideas ultimately caused Russell to shrink from him. Russell says in *Portraits From Memory* (1956), 'it was only gradually that we discovered that we differed from each other more than we differed from the Kaiser.' At the time however, Russell thought so highly of Lawrence's opinions that he thought of killing himself after some harsh criticism from Lawrence, as he admits in *Portraits From Memory*. In early 1916 he broke off the friendship, and years after Lawrence's death wrote an essay about him with a pen dipped in vinegar.

Lady Ottoline Morrell

'The Rainbow'   Lawrence completed *The Rainbow* at Greatham. Edward Garnett had not approved of it, and his relations with Lawrence frayed; Duckworth, the publishers for whom Garnett worked, did not bring out the book. It appeared under the auspices of Methuen in September, while the Lawrences were living in the Vale of Health, at Hampstead. Two years earlier the critics had generally accepted *Sons and Lovers,* that story of a young man's love affairs in the colliery country and his inability to break away from his mother; but now they fell upon *The Rainbow,* the story of a Midlands farm family and one of its members, Ursula Brangwen, whose search for identity took her through some erotic experiences that shocked the vestigial Victorianism of the reviewers. In November a police-court magistrate declared the book obscene, fined the

1 Byron Villas, Hampstead, where the Lawrences lived from August to December 1915

Lawrence gave this drawing, which he made in Sussex, to Viola Meynell on 2 March 1915. It shows Eastwood rising on the hill in the distance, with a hayfield and the coal wagons of Barber, Walker & Co. in the foreground

Current Literature
BOOKS IN GENERAL

LAST Saturday, at Bow Street, Mr. D. H. Lawrence's new novel *The Rainbow* was brought before the bench and sentenced to death. Who lodged an information against the book I don't know. It is conceivable, at a time when the patriotism of our criminals must leave our policemen plenty of leisure, that some cultured constable may have got hold of the work and rushed to his superiors with it. But it is likelier that the prosecution was the work of some Society or individual set upon Mr. Lawrence's track by one of the violent attacks upon the book which appeared in the Press. Two of these attacks figured in court, those of Mr. James Douglas and Mr. Clement Shorter. The prosecution attached much importance to them and the magistrate blamed the publishers for not withdrawing the book as a direct result of these gentlemen's criticisms. And both these critics as well as counsel for the prosecution and the magistrate himself talked a good deal of hyperbolical nonsense.

* * *

Some qualification must be made with regard to Mr. Douglas and Mr. Shorter. Mr. Douglas is a man with a genius for invective which I myself heartily appreciate when

The New Statesman's report of the difficulties over *The Rainbow*. 'I can't come so near to them as to fight them. I have done with them. I am not going to pay any more out of my soul, even for the sake of beating them.' (Letter)

publisher, and ordered the destruction of all existing available copies of the book. Philip Morrell courageously brought the matter up twice in Parliament, questioning the legality of the proceedings, but he was smoothly muffled by the Home Secretary, Sir John Simon who, some twenty years later, appeased rather than muffled the Nazis.

The Rainbow was, and still is, an avant-garde novel. There is good reason to suspect, as Richard Aldington and others have pointed out, that the suppression was as much on account of the war as of obscenity. The British forces were not doing well on the Western Front in 1915, and recruiting lagged; in Lawrence's book, Ursula makes fun of the uniform of her lover, Skrebensky, who fights in the Boer War.

The original of Marsh Farm in *The Rainbow*. 'The house stood bare from the road, approached by a straight garden path, along which at spring the daffodils were thick in green and yellow. At the sides of the house were bushes of lilac and guelder-rose and privet, entirely hiding the farm buildings behind.' *(The Rainbow)*

Church Cottage, Cossall

Church Cottage, Cossall: the honeymoon cottage in *The Rainbow*. 'It was the cottage next the church, with dark yew-trees, very black old trees, along the side of the house and the grassy front garden; a red, squarish cottage with a low slate roof, and low windows.' (*The Rainbow*)

In writing *The Rainbow*, Lawrence broke new ground, seeing his material in a new way. It begins traditionally enough, somewhat in the manner of *Sons and Lovers*, with overtones of Thomas Hardy, but after a time it becomes an entirely different production, particularly in its representation of states of consciousness. At the beginning, *The Rainbow* is the chronicle of a farming family in the Midlands, the Brangwens; it is a story of the soil, told at times in almost Biblical rhythms. But the pace, the tone, the angle of vision, the philosophical values of the book, are all changed by the time the narrative focuses on a third-generation member of the family, Ursula, one of the first 'modern' women in fiction. Lawrence described Ursula's love affair with Anton Skrebensky in a

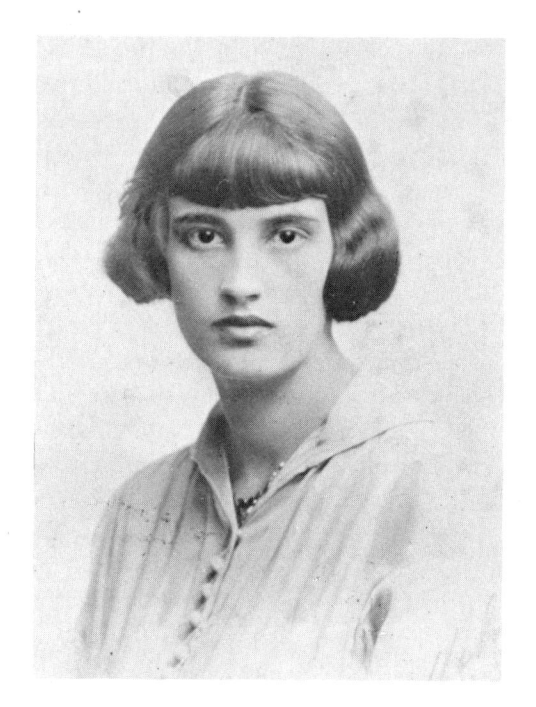

Minnie Lucie Channing (later Mrs Heseltine). 'She had beautiful eyes, flower-like, fully opened, naked in their looking at him. And on them there seemed to float a curious iridescence, a sort of film of disintegration, and sullenness, like oil on water.' (*Women in Love*)

candidly physical way that shocked the reviewers of 1915, and he also attempted to convey impressions of the consciousness during sexual ecstasy. One of the episodes that brought legal penalties upon the book was Ursula's experimental and unsatisfying erotic experience with one of her schoolmistresses, Winifred Inger; in those days lesbianism was a forbidden subject. 'Ursula lay still in her mistress's arms, her forehead against the beloved, maddening breast', and a moment later 'Ursula twined her body about her mistress.' But Ursula's attachment does not last, nor does that to Skrebensky, who represents the military, the Empire, and conventional standards; he becomes impotent before Ursula's intensity. At the end of the book, the girl sees the rainbow arching over the earth and envisages it as the promise of a new life: pettiness will be swept away before grandeur.

Lawrence had intended to go to America after the publication of *The Rainbow*, and he and Frieda had obtained passports; but the troubles over the novel delayed him. At the end of 1915, poor and embittered, they moved to the coast of Cornwall, where for nearly two years they lived in a cottage at Zennor. The stony fields and the black nights over the sea matched Lawrence's mood. He took parts left over from *The Sisters* and shaped them into *Women in Love*, continuing the story of Ursula. He added caricatures of some of his new friends, including Lady Ottoline, who appears as the rather monstrous Hermione

'Women in Love' Roddice, slave to her will. For two of the characters, Gerald Crich and Ursula's sister, Gudrun Brangwen, Lawrence borrowed characteristics from Murry and Katherine Mansfield. Murry was hardly recognizable because Lawrence gave Gerald the outer casing of the owner of Lamb Close House, Eastwood: Thomas (later Sir Thomas) Philip Barber (1876-1961). Lamb Close is called Shortlands in the book, as the Morrells' Garsington is called Breadalby.

The action of *Women in Love* takes place some years after that of *The Rainbow*. Ursula is at last to find a measure of fulfilment in Rupert Birkin, a somewhat Lawrence-like figure who is an inspector of schools. But first Birkin has to escape from the toils of Hermione and her will. This is, perhaps unconsciously, a reflection of Lawrence's will-driven mother, and of Jessie Chambers. Almost perversely, Lawrence often seemed drawn to women of this type, of which Mabel Dodge Luhan, in New Mexico, was a later example. But he caricatured the type most fully in the character of Hermione, who eventually loses Birkin to

Lawrence's cottage at Higher Tregerthen, Zennor. 'What we have found is a two-roomed cottage, one room up, one down, with a long scullery.... It is just under the moors, on the edge of the few rough stony fields that go to the sea. It is quite alone, as a little colony.' (Letter)

Sir Thomas Philip Barber.
'... fair, good-looking, healthy, with a great reserve of energy.'
(*Women in Love*)

Ursula. Meanwhile, the young mine-owner Gerald Crich has taken up with Gudrun Brangwen, who like her sister has become a teacher. The two couples —there is a strange bond between Gerald and Birkin, most apparent in their intense wrestling scene—go together to the Continent; Birkin marries Ursula, but Gerald and Gudrun forego the legal ceremony.

In the snowy mountains of the Austrian Tyrol, Gudrun begins a love affair with a cynical little sculptor, Loerke, who sells his work to adorn industrial buildings, a sure sign of Lawrence's disapprobation. Not that Lawrence approves of Gerald, who in operating his mines represents the mechanical, anti-human spirit Lawrence loathed. In this novel, incidentally, he was apparently drawing upon myth: as first pointed out in *The Life and Works of D. H. Lawrence* (1951), Loerke seems a modern version of the evil figure in Scandinavian legend whose name was Loki; Gudrun, in the Eddic version of the Siegfried story, is Siegfried's mate, and the name Gerald is an old Teutonic word for spear-bearer, the warrior. Lawrence was apparently giving the conclusion of his book a *Götterdämmerung* parallel, ending with the half-symbolic

Southwell Minster. 'The rigid, sombre, ugly cathedral was settling under the gloom of the coming night, as they entered the narrow town. . . .'
(*Women in Love*)

death of Gerald (who in the novel represents the cold, materialistic, 'northern' way of life) on the icy slopes of the Tyrolese Alps. Gerald has denied the kind of life envisaged by Birkin, who utters some of Lawrence's most important statements of his values. One of these, repeated throughout the book by means of symbols, is of opposition to mechanization and industrialism; another is Lawrence's philosophy of personal relationships. As Birkin tells Ursula, 'What I want is a conjunction with you . . . an equilibrium, a pure balance of the two single beings:—as the stars balance each other.' Later, when she asserts that he has said he wanted submission, he explains, 'I did not say, nor imply, a satellite. I meant two single equal stars balanced in conjunction—'. And this is a way of life. This is what Lawrence was working out for himself on the dark and stony Cornish coast.

John Middleton Murry
c. 1916. 'I think that one day—
before so very long—we shall
come together again, this time on
a living earth, not in the
destructive world of going apart.
I believe we shall do things
together, and be happy.' (Letter)

Murry and Katherine Mansfield had, at Lawrence's urging, reluctantly gone to bleak Cornwall in 1916 from southern France, where they had been happy in the sun at Bandol. Lawrence, as he walked across the Cornish moors with Murry, wanted the two of them to seal some kind of sacramental friendship—one of the themes of *Women in Love*—a rather incomprehensible ceremony of blood-brotherhood that seems to have been mystical rather than sexual. The idea baffled and terrified Murry. Relations between the couples became strained, and soon 'the Murrys' (who were finally to marry in 1918) left for another part of Cornwall and eventually for London. Lawrence meanwhile seems to have realized some kind of blood-brothership with a local farmer, as described in *Kangaroo* (1923). One long section of *Kangaroo* ('The Nightmare') reports some of Lawrence's wartime experiences in Cornwall. From this, his letters, and the memoirs of some of his friends, the tormenting events of the period can be partly reconstructed. The singular-looking, red-bearded man was an object of suspicion to most of the Cornish people: he spoke out boldly against the war, he loathed the new Lloyd George government, and he had a German wife. At night at home the couple defiantly sang German *Lieder,* mixing with them some ancient Celtic songs which the local Celts, spying in the bushes around

Persecution

Hilda Doolittle (H.D.), the wife of Richard Aldington. Photograph taken *c.* 1949

the cottage, thought were also German. When the Lawrences left the cottage it would be searched, and they were in other ways, officially and unofficially, hounded. With barely enough food to subsist on, they were accused of provisioning German submarines off the coast. At last, in October 1917, they were officially ordered to leave Cornwall, to stay out of all seaside areas, and to report regularly to the police wherever they were. They went to London, with Lawrence's heart full of black hatred for his countrymen and the mass bullying that went on everywhere at the time.

Mountain Cottage

In late 1917, the American poet H.D. (Hilda Doolittle) lent the Lawrences her room in Mecklenburgh Square while her husband, Richard Aldington, was away on the Western Front. In London they met H.D.'s American friend, Dorothy Yorke, whom Lawrence was to portray as Josephine Ford in *Aaron's Rod*. By the end of the year, Lawrence and Frieda had moved to a mountainside cottage which his sister Ada had rented for them in the Derbyshire highlands: 'It is in the darkish midlands, on the rim of a steep valley, looking over the darkish, folded hills—exactly the navel of England, and feels exactly that.'

Mountain Cottage, Middleton-by-Wirksworth, Derbyshire. 'It is in the darkish Midlands, on the rim of a steep deep valley, looking over the darkish, folded hills—exactly the navel of England, and feels exactly that.' (Letter)

At Mountain Cottage c. 1918: *(above left)* Enid Hopkin, Dorothy Yorke, Lawrence and W. E. Hopkin, *(above right)* Ada Lawrence Clarke, W. E. Hopkin, Edward Clarke, Frieda Lawrence, Mrs W. E. (Sallie) Hopkin, Gertrude Cooper (?), Lawrence and, on the right, an unknown man. Lawrence and Frieda *(below left)* at Grimsbury Farm, near Newbury *(below right)* c. 1919. '. . . a little homestead, with ancient wooden barn and low-gabled farmhouse, lying just one field removed from the edge of the wood.' *(The Fox)*

Maurice Magnus. '... spruce and youngish in his deportment, very pink-faced, and very clean, very natty, very alert, like a sparrow painted to resemble a tom-tit.' (Introduction to *Memoirs of the Foreign Legion*)

The Lawrences stayed there until after the war, occasionally visited by Dorothy Yorke or going to see friends in Berkshire, stopping off in London on the way. Lawrence was called up several times for physical examinations for military service, but was rejected because of his weak chest. In *Kangaroo* he describes how he hated being handled by the medical men.

During these years he published very little, and his principal writing activity was his essays on American authors, published in 1923 as *Studies in Classic American Literature*. Towards the end of the war Lawrence often thought with longing of America, but also of the South Pacific, about which Herman Melville had written. In those last unhappy years he was to spend in England, Lawrence yearned for lands of gleaming sunshine and bright colours.

Passports finally arrived. In October 1919, Frieda, whose father was now dead, went to Germany to visit her mother. In November Lawrence travelled by train to Italy, having arranged to meet Frieda in Florence. While waiting for her he spent some time with Norman Douglas, bluff and red-faced and white haired, who had picked up a strange American friend, Maurice Magnus, who was vaguely connected with literature and the theatre. As Lawrence described him, 'he stuck out his front rather tubbily, like a bird, and his legs seemed

Norman Douglas and Maurice Magnus

Norman Douglas by Desmond Harmsworth 1933. 'He must have been very handsome in his day, with his natural dignity, and his clean-shaven strong square face. But now his face was all red and softened and inflamed, his eyes had gone small and wicked under his bushy grey brows. Still he has a presence.' (*Aaron's Rod*)

Norman Douglas and Giuseppe (Pino) Orioli hiking in Austria *c.* 1932

to perch behind him, as a bird's do.' Lawrence drew a full-length portrait in the introduction he wrote for Magnus's posthumous book, *Memoirs of the Foreign Legion,* 'by M. M.'. When it came out in 1924, several years after Magnus's death and after much prodding of publishers by Lawrence, Douglas wrote a furious pamphlet accusing Lawrence of maligning Magnus as well as Douglas, and of making money out of the former's drab little report of his rather incredible time in the Foreign Legion—money which Douglas said should have gone to him as Magnus's literary executor. Lawrence, 'weary of being slandered', crushed Douglas with a letter to the *New Statesman* which explained that Magnus's creditors were being paid first out of the proceeds. Lawrence also quoted a 1921 letter from Douglas which said, 'By all means do what you like with the M.S.' and added (the italics are Douglas's), *'Pocket all the cash yourself.'* This should have put an end to a celebrated literary quarrel, particularly since Lawrence and Douglas later became friends again, but there is a Douglas cult that keeps up the fight. As late as 1954 its members were attacking Richard Aldington for *Pinorman,* his candid but amusing and satirical biography of Douglas and the Florentine bookseller, Giuseppe ('Pino') Orioli.

Italy   Soon after Frieda arrived in Italy, she and Lawrence went briefly to Rome and then to a farm in the mountains above Caserta. Since this was too cold, they moved on to Capri, arriving in time for Christmas. Lawrence remembered those icy mountains, however, and used them for the ending of his novel *The Lost Girl* (1920). On Capri, the Lawrences met the popular novelist Compton Mackenzie, who treated them cordially, though Lawrence wrote of him satirically in his letters at the time and later portrayed him in an uncomplimentary way in two later short stories (*The Man Who Loved Islands* and *Two Blue Birds*). From Capri, Lawrence wrote a cruel letter to Katherine Mansfield, saying 'I loathe you. You revolt me stewing in your consumption.' To Lawrence, Capri was 'a stew-pot of semi-literary cats', but he and Frieda stayed there two months. He once returned to the mainland, to visit Magnus at the great monastery of Monte Cassino, of which Lawrence has left unforgettable pictures in his introduction to the *Foreign Legion* book. Lawrence had intended to stay a week and absorb the life of the monastery, but he could stand only two days of Magnus's squeaking self-pity.

Lawrence and Frieda with Pino Orioli in Florence *c.* 1928. '... the broad and thick-set Italian ... in whom I can trust.'
(For a Moment)

Philip Heseltine. 'He was like a Christ in a Pietà. The animal was not there at all, only the heavy, broken beauty.... The fireglow fell on his heavy, rather bowed shoulders, he sat slackly crouched on the fender, his face was uplifted, weak, perhaps slightly disintegrate, and yet with a moving beauty of its own.' (*Women in Love*)

During that year of 1920, Lawrence's new American publisher, Thomas Seltzer, finally brought out *Women in Love*. A court action against the novel failed. Compton Mackenzie's English publisher, Martin Secker, launched the book in London in 1921. Lady Ottoline Morrell, who knew years before of the portrait of herself in the book, had long been estranged from the Lawrences. The composer Philip Heseltine ('Peter Warlock'), who appeared as Halliday in the story, bluffed Secker out of fifty pounds for 'damages'. Beyond all these considerations, *Women in Love,* with its profound exploration of human relationships, its many-sided portrait of a region, and its magnificent prose, is regarded by many critics as Lawrence's best novel.

Mrs Boris de Croustchoff, Judith Wood and Philip Heseltine

At the time of his return to the Mediterranean, then, Lawrence was re-established as a novelist; and, under the touch of southern sunlight he began to write prodigiously, producing poems, travel books, and fiction in abundance, as well as essays such as those of his two volumes of what he called his 'poly-analytics', *Psychoanalysis and the Unconscious* (1921) and *Fantasia of the Unconscious* (1922). In these books Lawrence attacked Freud, to whom he was nevertheless somewhat indebted, and in their pages he frequently manifested common sense (his statements about family relationships), though occasionally uttering nonsense (his assertion of belief in the 'lost continent' of Atlantis). Even work he had left unfinished was completed at this time, including the novel *The Lost Girl* (1920), which Lawrence had begun before the war, intending to call it *The Insurrection of Miss Houghton*. It was this book above all that re-established Lawrence as a publishable writer, for it won the James Tait Black Memorial Prize of Edinburgh University, the only official honour he was to be given during his lifetime; like Joyce and Proust he was ignored by the Nobel Prize committee. In *The Lost Girl,* Lawrence tells the story of Alvina Houghton,

'The Lost Girl'

Compton (now Sir Compton) Mackenzie in 1912. '... one feels the generations of actors behind him and can't be quite serious.' (Letter)

native of Woodhouse, obviously Eastwood, where her father operates the shop called Manchester House, based on the London House owned by a man named James Cullen. In boyhood Lawrence had observed Cullen, a dandy amid the colliers, but one who failed to make a success of selling finery to their wives. In completing the novel after the war, Lawrence made Alvina run off with an Italian actor, whom she marries and accompanies to Italy—as noted earlier, the novel ends in the frozen mountains above Caserta.

But Lawrence himself abandoned them for the warmth of Capri and, later, for the glamour of Sicily. This escape from England after the Armistice was a great release for him. He had three such occasions of release in his life, each connected with a voyage to Italy and the start of a new phase of his writing. The first period of his career as an author ended when he completed *Sons and*

Lovers on the shores of Lago di Garda in 1912, a few months after he had gone to Italy. All his earlier work had been concerned with the Midlands except *The Trespasser,* which swung between the south London suburbs and the Isle of Wight. En route to Italy in 1912, Lawrence wrote a few sketches of Germany, but his new life really began when he and Frieda crossed the Alps. In that last draft of *Sons and Lovers* he was also casting off the shackles of the past, and he began work on the books that were to become *The Rainbow* and *Women in Love*.

Similarly, at the end of 1919 and in the autumn of 1925, a return to Italy meant a new stimulus to his writing and, in each instance, the beginning of a new literary period. In 1925 he had exhausted his North American material—after he left New Mexico and Mexico he rarely wrote of them again—and the continent had exhausted him. In the year after he came back to Italy, he began writing the novel of his last phase, *Lady Chatterley's Lover,* and those last years of his life were partly spent on the Mediterranean coast of France. But this was a dying Lawrence—by contrast, the man who went south in November 1919 was a man making a new beginning after the war years in England. It will be remembered that he had returned from Italy with Frieda after her divorce had come through, and in time to be married barely a fortnight before the war broke out. Even during the first stages of the war they had contemplated returning to Italy, but that proved impracticable; later they had, for a time, considered going to America. But during most of the war, Lawrence (as we have seen) was virtually a captive: he spent the greater part of the last years of the war and the time just afterwards in his native Midlands, where he was unhappy and wrote little. But that voyage to the South, and the residence there, were an explosive release. Indeed, Lawrence's discoveries and rediscoveries of the bright South are somewhat comparable to the experience of Van Gogh, as described by Lewis Mumford in *Technics and Civilization*:

> In his early pictures he absorbed and courageously faced the most sinister parts of his environment: he painted the gnarled bodies of the miners, the almost animal stupor of their faces, bent over the bare dinner of potatoes, the eternal blacks, grays, dark blues, and soiled yellows of their poverty-stricken homes. Van Gogh identified himself with this sombre, forbidding routine: then, going to France, which had never entirely succumbed to the steam engine and large-scale production, which still retained its agricultural villages and its petty handicrafts, he found himself quickened to revolt against the deformities and deprivations of the new industrialism. In the clear air of Provence, Van Gogh beheld the visual world with a sense of intoxication deepened by the black denial he had known so long: the senses, no longer blanketed and muffled by smoke and dirt, responded in shrill ecstasy. The fog lifted: the blind saw: colour returned.

The Bay of Taormina, Sicily. 'This is the dawn-coast of Sicily. Nay, the dawn-coast of Europe. Steep, like a vast cliff, dawn-forward.' *(Sea and Sardinia)* ▶

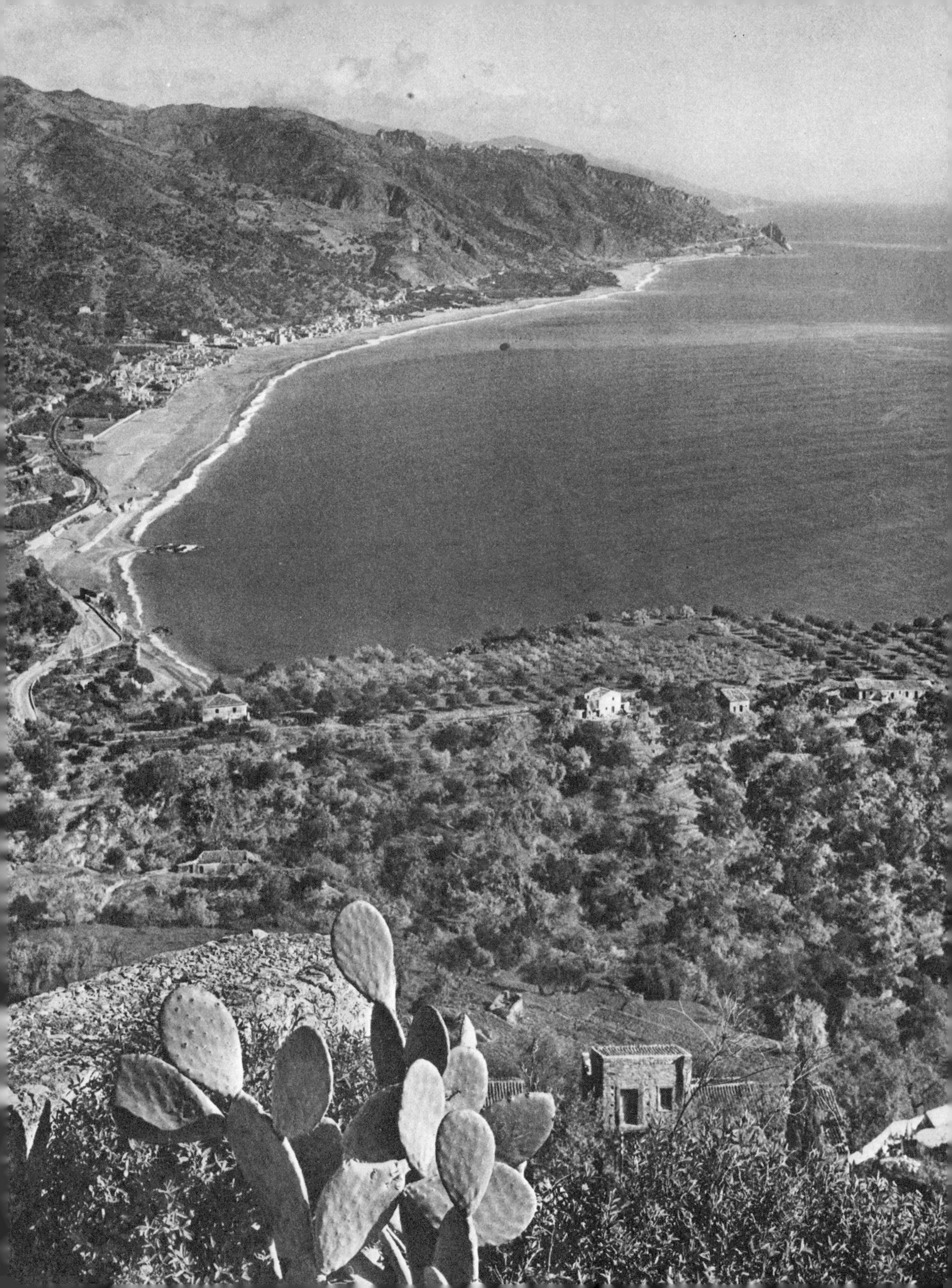

A portrait of Lawrence painted by Jan Juta at Taormina in 1920. 'He said in his heart, the day his beard was shaven he was beaten, lost. He identified it with his isolate manhood.' *(Kangaroo)*

Villa Fontana Vecchia, Taormina. 'We've got a nice big house, with fine rooms and a handy kitchen, set in a big garden, mostly vegetables, green with almond trees, on a steep slope at some distance above the sea . . . . It is beautiful, and green, green, and full of flowers.' (Letter)

Taormina   At the beginning of March 1920, the Lawrences moved to Taormina, Sicily, where they lived for two years amid olive groves and lemon trees at an old villa called Fontana Vecchia. Magnus soon followed them there, intimating that he had some bills which he expected Lawrence to pay. Lawrence did so, with irritation, and over Frieda's protests. They saw Magnus again during a visit to Malta, where Lawrence met several of his fellow creditors who, after Magnus's death, seemed to hold Lawrence responsible for the dead man's debts. It was after their return to Taormina that the Lawrences heard that Magnus had killed himself. His activities as a swindler had finally come to the attention of the police, and, when they closed in on him, he took hydrocyanic acid. Lawrence who heard that Magnus was an illegitimate offspring, by a Jewish woman, of the Hohenzollerns, realized that by giving him half of his own money, he could have kept the little parasite alive. But he had no regrets that he hadn't done so, for Magnus was an exploiter of the pity he aroused in others. Yet Lawrence found something heroic in the man's arrogance: 'He was a strange, quaking little star.'

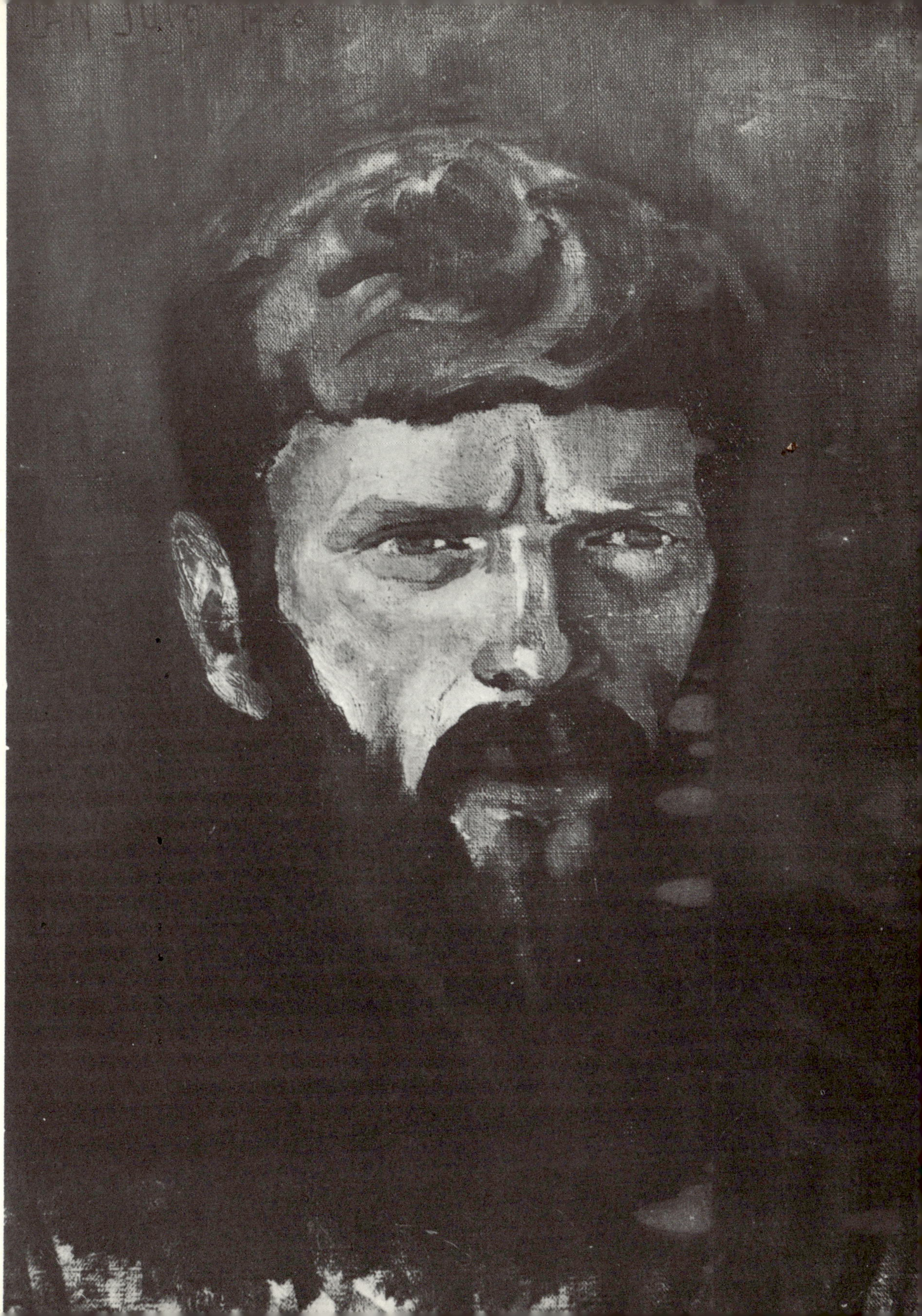

'Aaron's Rod'

During his two years' residence at Taormina, Lawrence made several trips to the European mainland, to Venice, to the Austrian Alps, and to visit Frieda's mother at Baden-Baden. A journey to one of the Mediterranean islands resulted in his brightly coloured travel book *Sea and Sardinia* (1921). At Taormina he wrote many of the poems of *Birds, Beasts and Flowers,* including *Snake,* which describes his encounter at a water-trough with 'one of the lords of life'. In 1921 Lawrence finished *Aaron's Rod,* published in the following year. Set in England and Italy, it was the first of his 'leadership' novels, revealing his interest in one of the acute problems of the modern world.

In the story, Aaron Sisson, who is a miners' checkweighman—a job superior to that of the colliers—becomes weary of his existence with his wife and children, and sets out for parts unknown. An experienced flautist, he becomes a member of a symphony orchestra in London and meets a Lawrence-like man, Rawdon Lilly, whom he follows to Florence. There Aaron has a love affair with an

Villa Becker, Val Salice, Turin. '. . . great luxury—rather nice people, really—but my stomach, my stomach, it has a bad habit of turning a complete somersault when it finds itself in the wrong element, like a dolphin in the air.' (Letter)

Dorothy Yorke, 1917. '... a cameo-like girl with hair done tight and bright in the French mode. She had strangely-drawn eyebrows, and her colour was brilliant.... Her movements were very quiet and well bred; but perhaps too quiet, they had the dangerous impassivity of the Bohemian, Parisian or American, rather than English.' *(Aaron's Rod)*

American woman married to an Italian count, but she does not fulfil him. He feels increasingly drawn towards Lilly, a prophetic man whom Aaron sees as something of a leader. Aaron's past life and part of his deepest self are broken off when his flute (his 'rod') is shattered by a bomb explosion in a cafe at a time of political upheaval. Lilly tells Aaron that in looking for a leader men often want merely an instrument to which they can be subservient; men and women must realize their own true selves and must submit only to a greater, heroic spirit. When, at the end of the book, Aaron asks whom he should submit to, Lilly says, 'Your soul will tell you.' Lawrence in planning the book had at one time intended to send Aaron to Monte Cassino at the end, but finally decided on a more secular conclusion.

Harwood (left), Achsah and Earl Brewster. 'I would like you and Achsah Brewster and the child to settle somewhere near. I would rather dig a little, and tend a few fruit-trees with you, than meditate with you. I would rather we did a bit of quite manual work together—and spent our days in our own solitude and labour.' (Letter)

The Brewsters   Revisiting Capri during his stay at Taormina, Lawrence met an American couple who were to remain his staunch friends for the rest of his life: Earl and Achsah Brewster, who had a young daughter named Harwood. Lawrence met the Brewsters, who were painters, after someone thought that Mrs Brewster's portrait of St Francis looked like Lawrence and brought him to see it. The Brewsters, who had expected to meet a ravaged and tormented man, were delighted to find him bright and full of life and laughter. They invited him to visit them in Ceylon, where they were going, and to bring his wife, then with her mother in Germany.

Kandy Lake and the Temple of the Sacred Tooth. 'Months spent in holy Kandy, in Ceylon, the holy of holies of southern Buddhism, had not touched the great psyche of materialism and idealism which dominated me.' *(New Mexico)*

In February 1922, the Lawrences sailed for Ceylon, where they stayed a month with the Brewsters in their bungalow in the hills above the Kandy Lake. Earl Brewster went each morning to study Pali at a Buddhist monastery; Lawrence, who had earlier expressed an interest in Buddhism, refused to accompany him. The afternoons were ferociously hot, and Lawrence became ill ('never felt so sick in my life'), but in the evenings he would join the Brewsters and Frieda in singing old ballads and acting charades. While in Ceylon he wrote a notable poem, *Elephant,* which described the ceremonial procession for the Prince of Wales (later the Duke of Windsor). Lawrence a

M. L. (Mollie) Skinner, co-author with Lawrence of *The Boy in the Bush*

few years later put the Brewsters into a satirical little story called *Things,* about wandering Americans who study 'Indian thought' and collect bric-a-brac all over the world. He assured the Brewsters that they were not the originals of the characters in the story, though they obviously were; but they were too good-natured to take offence.

Australia   Early in May the Lawrences arrived in Western Australia, where they met the nurse, Mollie Skinner, whose novel about that region Lawrence was later to revise; it appeared in 1924 as *The Boy in the Bush,* by D. H. Lawrence and M. L. Skinner. In late May Lawrence and Frieda passed through Sydney and moved into a cottage on the coast at Thirroul, New South Wales, where they stayed for nearly three months. Here Lawrence wrote *Kangaroo,* the second of his 'leadership' novels. On 10 August the Lawrences at last sailed for the United States, for San Francisco, on a ship that touched at Papeete, Tahiti, as well as at Katherine Mansfield's native Wellington, New Zealand, from where, a little less than a year before she died, Lawrence sent her a postcard in spite of their broken friendship.

Lawrence, Laura Forrester and Frieda *(above left)* at Wyewurk *(above right)*, Thirroul, New South Wales, in 1922. *(Below)* Lawrence, Laura Forrester and Frieda in the foreground with Mrs William Marchbanks standing behind them

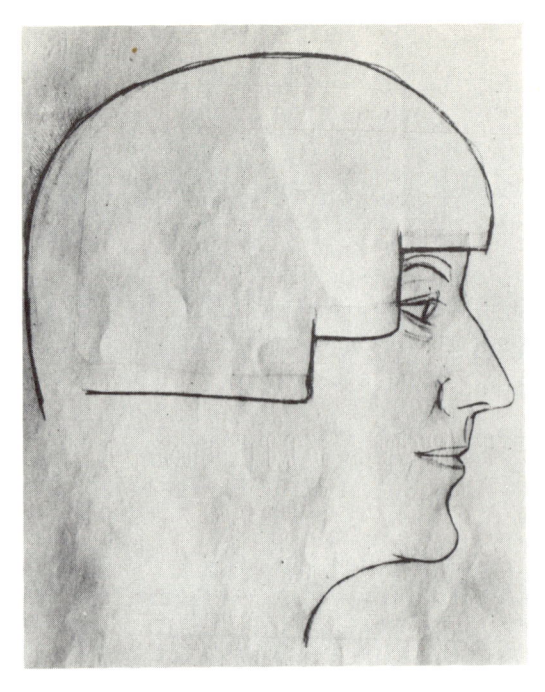

Mabel Dodge Luhan. '... is very "generous", wants to be "good" and is very wicked, has a terrible will-to-power, you know—she wants to be a witch and at the same time a Mary of Bethany at Jesus's feet—a big, white crow, a cooing raven of ill-omen.' (Letter)

Taos and Mabel Dodge Sterne

He and Frieda were going to America because they had been invited to Taos, New Mexico, by Mrs Mabel Dodge Sterne, later Mrs Luhan, a wealthy hunter of celebrities who felt that Lawrence could express in verse and prose the wonder she felt in New Mexico. She had settled there after a girlhood in Buffalo, New York, after what she called 'European experiences' in Paris and Florence, and after attempting to startle Greenwich Village. Lawrence had been warned against her, but was slowly, inevitably drawn towards Taos. Mrs Sterne had willed him to come: 'not prayer, but command'.

During the months when Lawrence hesitated over going to Taos, Mabel Sterne pitched her thoughts across space to compel him towards her. She told her Indian-buck lover, Tony Luhan, that the foreign man would bring helpful magic to the pueblo, and she persuaded him to join her in luring Lawrence and Frieda to New Mexico.

When at last they arrived at Lamy, the railway station near Santa Fe, Mrs Sterne and Tony were there to greet them. It was 10 September 1922, the eve of Lawrence's thirty-seventh birthday. The ample Frieda and the frail, red-bearded Lawrence descended from the train to meet the square little woman and her massive, braided Indian. 'Frieda', Mrs Sterne recorded in one of her moments of grotesque candour, 'immediately saw Tony and me sexually.' Mrs Sterne meanwhile felt her womb rouse 'to reach out and take' Lawrence.

(Above left) Lawrence and Frieda with Indians in New Mexico *c.* 1923

(Above right) Mabel Dodge Luhan's former residence at Taos. 'The big house is about 200 yards away—an adobe pile. I don't much like being on the grounds of a *padrona*: but Mabel Sterne is quite generous .... Whether I *really* like it is another matter. It is all an experience. But one's heart is never touched at all—neither by landscape, Indians, or Americans.' (Letter)

Willard Johnson and Witter Bynner with Lawrence at Santa Fe, New Mexico, 1923

The Indian drove them across the rocky desert to Santa Fe in the dark of early evening. It was too late to go on to Taos, so the Lawrences stayed in Santa Fe that night, in the little house of Witter Bynner the poet, who disliked Lawrence on sight. Nearly thirty years later, with Lawrence long dead, Bynner wrote one of the less friendly memoirs of him, *Journey With Genius*. Lawrence for his part said prophetically in a 1926 letter than Bynner was 'a sort of belated mosquito'.

On the morning after his arrival, Lawrence felt at once the power of the scenery: 'The moment I saw the brilliant, proud morning shine high up over the deserts of Santa Fe, something stood still in my soul, and I started to attend.' The magnificent, high-up day, with its 'eagle-like royalty', made the old world that Lawrence had known fade away before the spell of the new.

In saying that New Mexico was the greatest experience from the outside world he had ever had, Lawrence was not referring to people; unluckily, his new life could not be spent uninterruptedly with scenery. On that first morning in New Mexico Mrs Sterne had her Indian take them all over to Taos, where she put the Lawrences into an adobe house near her own. They went to supper

Lawrence's house in Chapala 1923. 'We've got a house here—very nice—green trees—a Mexican Isabel to look after us—a big lake of Chapala outside. . . . ' (Letter)

Lawrence c. 1920

at Mrs Sterne's hacienda that was stuffed with the paraphernalia she had accumulated in Europe—the kind which Lawrence would later make fun of in his story *Things*. In the dim, sunken dining-room, candles flickered amid bronzes, but the setting only inspired Lawrence to comment 'It's like one of those nasty little temples in India!'

Soon the hostess' frontier sophistication began to weary Lawrence: 'Too much Mabel Sterne and suppers and motor drives and people dropping in.' Before Lawrence had time to catch his breath, Mrs Sterne hustled him away with Tony, to see Indian dances at the Apache reservation. Lawrence later learned to like these dances, but the first ones he saw seemed to him like a solemnly played comic opera; he felt that the country was weird and that he was a stranger.

View from the mountains above Taos. 'I think New Mexico was the greatest experience from the outside world that I have ever had. It certainly changed me for ever.' *(New Mexico)*

While he and Tony were gone, Frieda eagerly unrolled the family secrets before Mrs Sterne. The two women contrived an intimacy that enraged Lawrence when he returned. But he proposed that he and Mrs Sterne work together on a book about her life. Frieda ('I did not want this') kept intruding with a vigorous broom, sweeping the floor fiercely and singing stridently. She succeeded in sweeping away the plans for collaboration. Ten years later, Mrs Sterne would tell her frenzied side of the story in *Lorenzo in Taos,* which has aptly been called *Lorenzo in Chaos.*

In the mountain autumn, Lawrence learned to ride horseback among the piñons and yellowing aspens, under the great cloud-broken skies. But Mrs Sterne continued to irritate him: 'A "culture-carrier", likes to play the patroness, hates the white world and loves the Indian out of hate, is very "generous", wants to be "good" and is very wicked, has a terrible will-to-power.'

At the beginning of December the Lawrences withdrew to a five-room log cabin at Del Monte ranch in the Sangre de Cristo range above Taos. They annoyed Mrs Sterne by bringing with them two Danish painters from the Taos

Lawrence at Kiowa
by Kai Gótzsche

art colony, who took a nearby cabin. Mrs Sterne had pointedly snubbed these men, Knud Merrild and Kai Gótzsche, who could now, when she came up for a visit, run off chuckling to hide among the trees with Lawrence.

   It was a savage winter, the mountains snow-heavy and the pines and spruces ice-packed; far below, a crooked line in the valley marked the Rio Grande. Lawrence had for a pet the dog named Bibbles—'little Walt-Whitmanesque bitch'—about which he wrote a poem. Once, when he kicked Bibbles in a rage, Merrild threatened him. But the winter ended peacefully enough, and in March the Lawrences, dodging Mrs Sterne, went through Taos to Lamy and then down to Mexico City.

Hotel Monte Carlo (the San Remo of *The Plumed Serpent*) where Lawrence stayed several times when he visited Mexico City

Lawrence at Lake Chapala in 1923

The pyramids at Teotihucán, Mexico

There Lawrence and Frieda stayed, as on later occasions, at the Hotel Monte Carlo, to be called the San Remo in *The Plumed Serpent:* 'rough, but it's kindly and human and not rotten.' The Lawrences went to see the pyramids at Teotihuacán, and visited other places in the vicinity before they finally moved on to Jalisco state. They rented a house in Chapala which was used for Kate's living quarters in *The Plumed Serpent* (1926). The Lawrences made a trip on Lake Chapala with Witter Bynner and other acquaintances on a boat that was pitched about by storms. The chalk-white lake became an important part of the scenery in *The Plumed Serpent,* which Lawrence began writing at Chapala in 1923.

View from Kiowa ranch. 'Ah! it was beauty, beauty absolute, at any hour of the day. . . .' *(St Mawr)*

Lawrence in 1923. 'Pan keeps on being reborn, in all kinds of strange shapes . . . . The Pan relationship, which the world of man once had with all the world, was better than anything man has now.' *(Pan in America)*

U.S.A. In July he and Frieda went to New York by way of New Orleans and Washington, and for a month stayed in a cottage at Union Hill, Dover, New Jersey. Lawrence made several trips to New York City to see his American publisher, Thomas Seltzer. The people in Union Hill recall Lawrence, and remember that Thomas Edison was frequently in the vicinity, trying to develop a synthetic rubber from a plot of milkweed which he had under cultivation near Lawrence's cottage. Local residents believe that the two men met and exchanged ideas.

On one of his trips to New York, Lawrence went to lunch at the Algonquin Hotel with Oswald Garrison Villard and the staff of *The Nation*. Two members of the British Labour Party were also guests. Joseph Wood Krutch, who was then on *The Nation*, remembers that Villard, after hearing what Labour would do to save the world, asked Lawrence what his remedy would be. With measured ferocity, Lawrence said, 'I thought, Mr Villard, you understood that I hoped it would go to pieces as rapidly and completely as possible.'

Frieda at this time wanted to return to Europe and Lawrence didn't; she went alone, in August, to Baden-Baden and London. It was the first real separation, a definite split, in the Lawrences' married life. Murry, who had founded *The Adelphi* in order to give Lawrence a forum, wanted him to come to England and take over the magazine; but Lawrence held back. He went to Los Angeles and, in September and October, travelled down the west coast of Mexico with Kai Götzsche, who wrote to his friend Knud Merrild that he thought Lawrence was from time to time insane, 'working himself up to will to go to England.' Lawrence meanwhile was rewriting, and considerably changing, Mollie

Lawrence drawn by
Knud Merrild c. 1923

Skinner's Australian novel, *The House of Ellis,* into *The Boy in the Bush.* After staying a month at Guadalajara, Jalisco, Lawrence in mid-November went to Mexico City and a few days later sailed from Vera Cruz for England. Frieda had cabled him imperatively to join her, and he had written from Guadalajara, 'I'll come back and say how do you do! to it all. I am glad if you have a good time with your flat and your children'—and he had added coldly, 'When I come we'll make a regular arrangement for you to have an income if you wish.'

Return to England

He hated the place when he saw it again. Murry recalled that he looked at London 'with a greenish pallor'; he might justifiably have been green-eyed if he had known that Frieda had proposed to Murry that they become lovers. Out of loyalty to Lawrence, Murry refused, in what he later wrote of in his journal as the 'great renunciation' of his life. Nearly seven years later, in Vence, the little town in France where Lawrence had died shortly before, Murry and Frieda at last became lovers, and he noted, 'With her, and for the first time in my life, I knew what fulfilment in love really meant.' But in 1923 he could only tell Frieda, 'No, my darling, I mustn't let Lorenzo down—I can't.'

The Hon. Dorothy Brett in New Mexico. '... try, try, try to get a real kindliness and wholeness.' (Letter)

Lawrence revisited his native Midlands and found the sooty industrialism depressing. He and Frieda had made peace and went to Baden-Baden together for two weeks in February 1924. The next month they returned to the United States, bringing with them the lone recruit Lawrence had been able to enlist for the ideal colony he wanted to found in the New Mexican mountains, the utopia he called Rananim from one of his friend Koteliansky's Hebrew songs. In London Lawrence had tried to persuade Murry and others to join him in creating a pantisocracy in the Rockies, but in an alcoholic 'Last Supper' scene at the Café Royal, all but one had refused. The single colonist was a painter, the Honourable Dorothy Brett, daughter of Viscount Esher and a friend of Lady Ottoline Morrell. Dorothy Brett was later (1933) to write one of the genuinely good memoirs of Lawrence: *Lawrence and Brett, A Friendship*.

The Hon. Dorothy Brett

Lawrence by Dorothy Brett

Kiowa   In March 1924 she and the Lawrences arrived at Taos, and in early May moved up into the Sangre de Cristo mountains to a small ranch Mabel Dodge (now Mrs Luhan) had given to Frieda, the ranch that was eventually called Kiowa. Lawrence hadn't enjoyed his stay in Taos. Mrs Luhan resented Dorothy Brett, who had an ear trumpet called Toby, which Mrs Luhan felt was a 'spy'. And two young house guests—a would-be writer named Clarence Thompson and a man who was later to be a distinguished student of Indian anthropology, Jaime de Angulo—became embroiled in the Lawrences' affairs. Lawrence and Frieda were glad to be up on the mountain; Brett took a house nearby. But no Rananim developed.

Kiowa ranch in the Sangre de Cristo mountains. '... the two cabins inside the rickety fence, the rather broken corral beyond, and behind all, tall, blue balsam pines, the round hills, the solid up-rise of the mountain flank....' *(St Mawr)*

(Below) The kitchen at Kiowa. 'We baked bread and roasted chickens in the oven—very good. We can bake twenty loaves of bread in half an hour in it.' *(Letter)*

Lawrence with Susan, his cow. Assisting him is Frieda's nephew, Friedel Jaffe. 'How can I equilibrate myself with my black cow Susan? ... There *is* a sort of relation between us. And this relation is part of the mystery of love....' *(Love Was Once A Little Boy)*

Inner chamber in
Palace II,
Mitla, Oaxaca

In October, accompanied by Dorothy Brett, the Lawrences went to Mexico City. In November they settled in a little house in Oaxaca, with their friend staying at a hotel. But she went back to Taos the following January, after Frieda announced thunderously that she didn't want any more of 'the Brett' and her curate-and-spinster relationship with Lawrence.

Tuberculosis   In February 1925 he finished *The Plumed Serpent.* After this he fell into a terrible illness, which a doctor in Mexico City said was tuberculosis. Lawrence for the remaining five years of his life never referred to his disease except as trouble with his 'broncs'. In early April he was back at Kiowa ranch, recuperating in the mountain sunlight. In September he left America for the last time, and at the end of the month he and Frieda arrived in England. After visiting

(Above) Mrs G. R. G. Conway, Lawrence and Frieda in Mexico City 1925

(Below) Lawrence examining pottery at Oaxaca, and talking to a Mexican Indian

(Above right) Lawrence and Frieda at a market; *(below)* with their landlord, Father Richards, in Oaxaca 1924/5. Lawrence is playing with Corsamin, the dog

Villa Bernarda, Spotorno. 'The village is not much to brag about — but the hills are fine and wild and the villa is above the houses and has a big vineyard garden.' (Letter)

D. H. Lawrence and Martin Secker, his English publisher, Spotorno 1925. 'Martin Secker is here . . . a nice gentle soul, without a thrill. . . .' (Letter)

London and crossing to Baden-Baden, they settled for the winter on the Italian Riviera, at Spotorno, near Genoa. There they rented the Villa Bernarda from an Italian army officer, a dark, vivacious little man, Angelo Ravagli, who twenty years after Lawrence's death was to marry Frieda. While at the Villa Bernarda, Frieda was visited by her two now grown daughters, Barbara and Elsa. Lawrence at one point went by himself to Capri for a while.

Angelo Ravagli. 'The *Tenente* still writes occasionally from Porto Maurizio, where he is transferred: rather lachrymose and forlorn.' (Letter)

Early in May 1926, the Lawrences moved to the house that was to be the most famous of all they had lived in, the Villa Mirenda, outside Florence, which they rented for two years. There was one more visit to England, which Lawrence still disliked, and he and Frieda returned from time to time to Baden-Baden and visited other parts of the continent. Frieda complained to friends at this time that her intermittently ill husband was now impotent.

At the Villa Mirenda Lawrence wrote his last novel, *Lady Chatterley's Lover*, which he arranged to have privately printed and circulated. Pino Orioli, in Florence, attended to many of the business details. The book was suppressed in England and the United States, some thirty years before the courts in those countries declared that it was not obscene and permitted it to be published unexpurgated. While he was working on the novel, Lawrence knew that he would be reviled for having written so candidly of love, but he had a message for the modern world, which he felt had become over-intellectualized and,

Villa Mirenda

through industrialism, inhumanly mechanized. He felt that modern men and women had broken 'the true pact between the body and soul': *Lady Chatterley's Lover* was a serious attempt to bring them back into a balanced relationship.

This, then, despite its reputation as a notable example of erotica, is essentially a philosophical book. Indeed, it is one of Lawrence's four major novels. The two most important—and this is a widely accepted critical estimate—are *The Rainbow* and *Women in Love,* with *Sons and Lovers* and *Lady Chatterley's Lover* at a somewhat lower level of excellence. *The Rainbow* and *Women in Love,* as the discussions of them have made evident, are certainly philosophical novels, at least novels of ideas. In them, Lawrence reached the peak of his imaginative writing; they represent the most harmonious balance between what he was trying to say and the way in which he said it. In other words, the ideas were more successfully embodied by the people, story, and language than in Lawrence's other books.

Lawrence reading *Lady Chatterley's Lover* to Reginald Turner, Norman Douglas and Pino Orioli at Orioli's home in Florence; painted from memory by Collingwood Gee in 1933

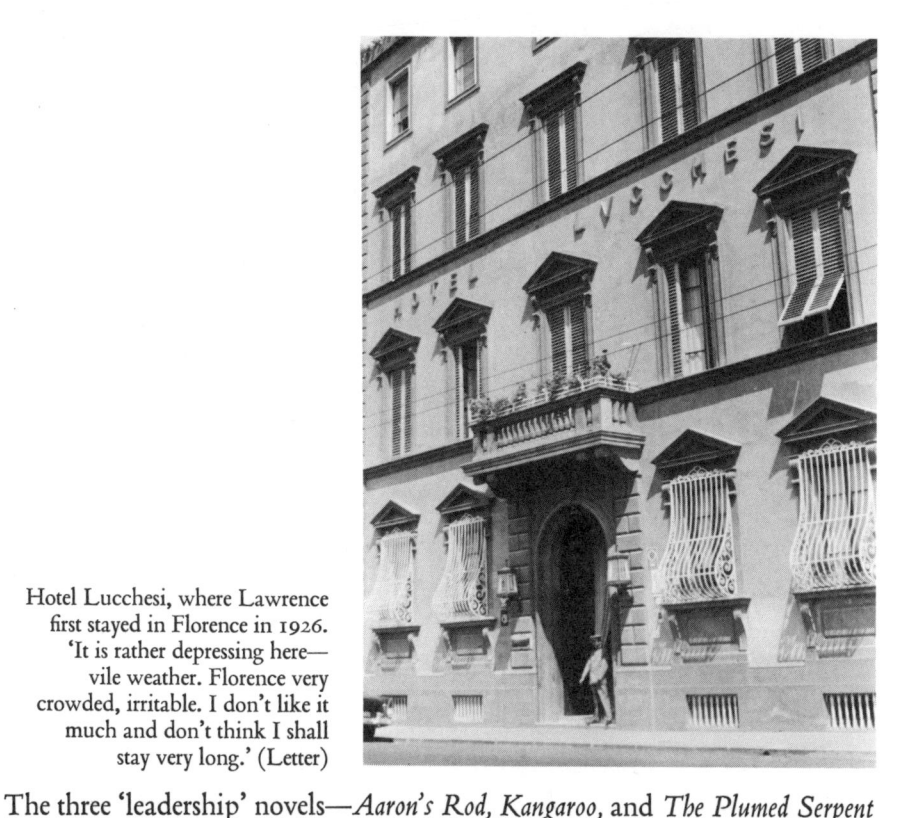

Hotel Lucchesi, where Lawrence first stayed in Florence in 1926. 'It is rather depressing here—vile weather. Florence very crowded, irritable. I don't like it much and don't think I shall stay very long.' (Letter)

The three 'leadership' novels—*Aaron's Rod, Kangaroo,* and *The Plumed Serpent*—are less effective in achieving such a balance. They are, however, magnificently written, and present luminous pictures of Italy, Australia, and Mexico. But *Aaron's Rod* is hardly a story; it is a succession of pictures of the modern world, ranging from England to Italy, with Aaron finally being magnetized by Lilly. In *Kangaroo,* the Lawrence-like man Richard Lovat Somers lives for a time on the Australian coast with his German-born wife Harriet, and meets the Sydney lawyer Ben Cooley, who has a physical resemblance to a kangaroo, from which he takes his nickname—a rather totemic figure. Somers, disgusted with Europe, particularly after suffering from war-time bullying in Cornwall, is for a while drawn to Kangaroo's secret political organization, the 'Diggers', which is not unlike some of the fascist groups whose manifestations Lawrence had witnessed in Italy. Somers is also attracted by the socialists, even then strong in Australia; they ask him, as a writer who is the son of a working-man, to take over their newspaper. But Somers rejects both the 'fascists' and socialists, and decides to stand by his own sacred individuality. (Lawrence, antagonistic to democracy, never seems to have realised that only a democracy makes such an attitude possible.)

The 'leadership' novels

Villa Mirenda, near Florence. 'We've taken this old and bare sort of farm-villa: or at least, the top half of it, for a year. But it costs very little, so we can just keep it as a *pied-à-terre*. It's very nice country, about seven miles out of Florence.' (Letter)

Kangaroo is wounded in a street riot between his faction and the socialists, and Somers leaves for San Francisco with the prophecy of the dying Kangaroo hanging over him: 'They'll kill you in America!' In *The Plumed Serpent* Lawrence went back on the principles of individualism expressed in *Kangaroo* and let his central character become part of a mystic movement, with political overtones, in Mexico. This central character was not, this time, a Lawrence-like man but rather a Frieda-like woman, Kate Leslie, who out of weariness with Europe goes to Mexico City. There she meets a somewhat Lawrence-like figure, glorified as one of the 'dark' people Lawrence tended to celebrate: Cipriano (emblematic name), General Viedma. He introduces Kate to his friend and associate, the mystic-demagogue Don Ramón Carrasco, who is attempting to revive the religion of the ancient god Quetzalcoatl (after whom Lawrence originally wanted to name the book). There are revivalist meetings, with Don Ramón acting as a kind of choirmaster as the peons gather in the plaza to chant the hymns of Quetzalcoatl, which have a strange resemblance to the songs of the miners' bethel in Lawrence's childhood. The revolution of Ramón and Cipriano is successful, but hardly convinces the reader, since it omits all politico-economic considerations and exists almost entirely in terms of primitive, hypnotic

Looking towards Villa Mirenda from the chapel of San Paolo. 'It's very pretty country—Tuscan—farms on green little hills, and pine woods fringing the ridges.' (Letter)

religion. Detractors of Lawrence have called this a fascist book, since most of the characters in it seem to 'think with their blood', like the Nazis; but Lawrence himself would never have been happy under a totalitarian dictatorship—what he seems to be doing in *The Plumed Serpent* is recommending a restoration of instinctual and religious values which have become lost in the world of industrialism. His desire to bring the instinctual into balance with the intellectual was greatly different from the philosophy of the Nazis. In terms of a credible story, however, the government-by-mysticism in *The Plumed Serpent* is not enough, as Kate herself seems to realize towards the end. Lawrence himself seems hardly to have believed in the story by that time, yet for a while after completing the book he felt that *The Plumed Serpent* was his masterpiece.

Maguey plant with organ cacti in the background, Mexico

Whatever its faults, it is certainly written magnificently: nowhere else is there such an intense and living picture of Mexico. Consider the scene in which Kate is sitting on the verandah of the house she has rented near one of the great inland lakes:

Morning! Brilliant sun pouring into the patio, on the hibiscus flowers and the fluttering yellow and green rags of the banana trees. Birds swiftly coming and going, with tropical suddenness. In the dense shadow of the mango grove, white-clad Indians going like ghosts. The sense of fierce sun and almost more impressive, of dark, intense shadow.

D. H. Lawrence

Lawrence's prose, often slapdash but always glowing with life, takes the reader physically into Mexico. And, as Kate sits there, 'silently appears an old man with one egg held up mysteriously, like some symbol'—and this is exactly right, on the surface a venerable merchant holding up part of his wares for display, yet underneath he is like a mystic messenger from beyond, from what Lawrence elsewhere called 'the fatal Greater Day of the Indians', as contrasted with 'the fussy, busy, lesser day of the white people'. Lawrence conveyed these ideas better in short stories, however, than in *The Plumed Serpent*. There is, for example, the unfinished fragment *The Flying Fish,* from which the few words quoted above are taken, and the purely symbolic story *The Woman Who Rode Away*. He was also more effective in expressing his ideas in travel sketches interspersed with reflection, such as those in *Mornings in Mexico*.

But in *Lady Chatterley's Lover* Lawrence was once again able, as in *The Rainbow* and *Women in Love*—though, it must be repeated, with somewhat smaller success—to convey ideas in terms of a novel. In the year he completed *Lady Chatterley,* 1928, he in effect repudiated the message of *The Plumed Serpent,* and indeed of the other 'leadership' novels, when he said in a letter, 'The leader

'Lady Chatterley's Lover'

Villa Mirenda. The window of Lawrence's room can be seen at the top of the photograph

of men is a back number. After all, at the back of the hero is the militant ideal: and the militant ideal or ideal militant seems to me also a cold egg . . . The leader-cum-follower relationship is a bore. And the new relationship will be some sort of tenderness, sensitive, between men and men and men and women, and not the one up one down, lead on I follow, *ich dien* sort of business.'

This leads directly to *Lady Chatterley's Lover,* which Lawrence at one time thought of calling *Tenderness.* He wrote three drafts of this book before turning it over to Orioli for the Florentine printing of 1928. At the Villa Mirenda, Lawrence sometimes worked on the novel in the tower, where he could look over the abrupt little hills of Tuscany, full of olive trees and orchards, to the brown sprawl of Florence. At other times he wrote on the sun-splashed terrace of the villa, or at the nearby chapel of San Polo (or San Paolo), where he scratched away with his pen in a wooded area of umbrella pines and olive trees, amid the rich flowers of the South. Nightingales in the trees made 'a most intensely and most indubitably male sound', and hunters went past, dressed not unlike the gamekeeper in Lawrence's novel. He noted that one of them wore

Under this tree at Villa Mirenda Lawrence wrote a considerable proportion of Lady Chatterley's Lover

'velvet corduroys, bandolier, cartridges, game-bag over his shoulder', and carried 'a gun in his hand'.

As Lawrence wrote the three versions of the story, the gamekeeper at first was a perky little communist named Parkin; but gradually the somewhat Lawrence-like Oliver Mellors took over. Mellors, like Lawrence, came from the people, and like Lawrence he could speak refined language when he wished, but would on occasion drop into Derbyshire 'broad' dialect. The early love affairs of Mellors, as he describes them, suggest Lawrence's with Jessie Chambers and Helen Corke. But the resemblance is not complete: Mellors has been an army officer, and his violent wife, the former Bertha Coutts, is certainly not based on Frieda. Interestingly, Lawrence had used a gamekeeper as a character in his

Villa Mirenda *(above)*
with Frieda and Lawrence
in the doorway *(below)*

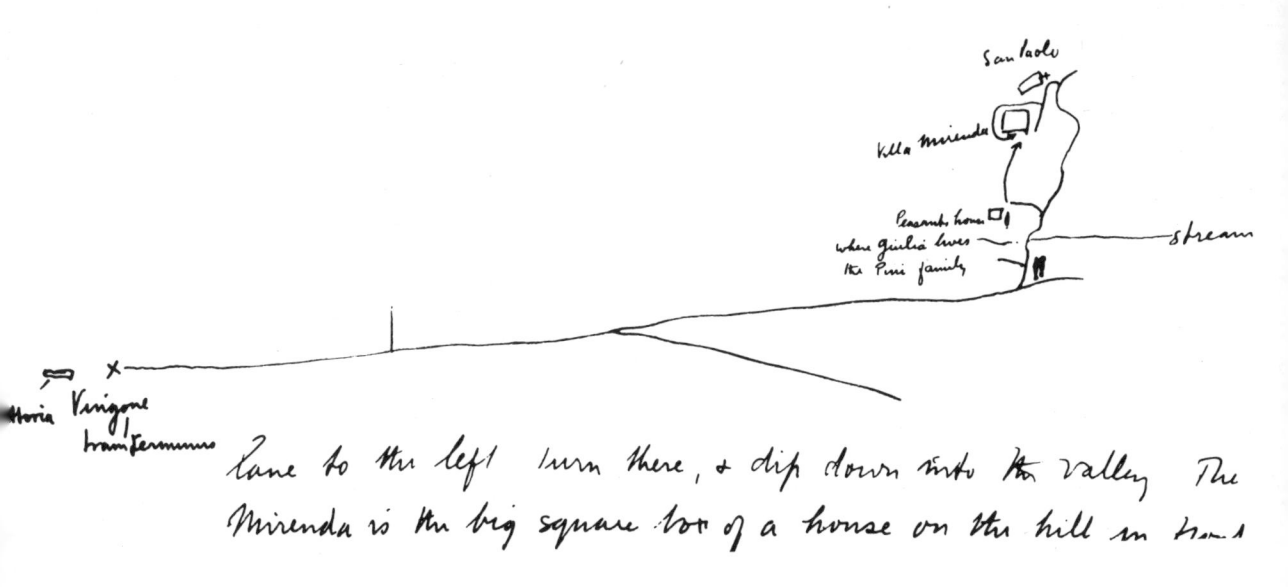

Part of Lawrence's letter to Enid Hilton, giving her directions on how to get to Villa Mirenda

first novel as well as his last: Annable, in *The White Peacock*, has correspondences with Mellors, including his early love affairs, but he plays little more than a choric role in that earlier book. Annable, in his relationship to the young people of *The White Peacock,* was probably suggested to Lawrence by the talkative gamekeeper Tregarva in Charles Kingsley's *Yeast*. But the portrait of Mellors has the benefit of Lawrence's nearly twenty years of experience between *The White Peacock* and *Lady Chatterley's Lover*.

The latter book is so well known that it hardly needs a summary, only an indication of what Lawrence was trying to accomplish in it. An important point to note is that, even before Sir Clifford Chatterley was sexually incapacitated by a wound received in the First World War, he had not taken 'the sex thing' very seriously in his month of marriage to Constance preceding his departure for the Western Front. Yet Connie, whose father calls her 'a bonny Scotch trout', is a normal young woman who wants fulfilment. After Clifford comes home—perhaps a bit too symbolically mechanized by his wheelchair—Connie has a love affair with the clever playwright Michaelis; but he is too intellectualized for either Connie or Lawrence, and at the same time his sex is dog-like; he is one of those men whom Connie thinks of as trotting, sniffing, and copulating. Mellors, on the contrary, is a man who has learned the sacredness of love. But he is also aware of the shame that many modern people feel about performing the act of love—the act which Mellors, in his efforts to burn such shame out of Connie, bluntly gives a four-letter name which throbbed on the page when the first readers of *Lady Chatterley* saw it there in 1928; it was then a secret expression, belonging to the gutter or the decoration of the public lavatory wall—but in a novel! Now that the battles of the 1950s and 60s have been won, that word and many others formerly forbidden appear frequently in novels. They are usually employed in a manner Lawrence would have considered obscene, as readers of his essays on pornography will discover.

Such words had appeared earlier in serious modern literature, in James Joyce's *Ulysses,* which first came out in its entirety in 1922 and at once became an item for tourists from English-speaking countries to take out of Paris and smuggle into their homelands. But after an American legal decision of 1933, *Ulysses* could be published lawfully and was no longer a contraband trophy. *Ulysses* was declared to be not obscene because it reflected life: the citizens of Dublin whom Joyce was writing about used the four-letter vocabulary in thought and speech, and it was only extreme realism (more properly, naturalism) to record what was in their minds and mouths. Yet Lawrence felt that Joyce was a dirty writer. His own intention in using such words was one of purification. This makes it all the more ironic that *Lady Chatterley's Lover* had to wait for more than a quarter of a century after the acceptance of *Ulysses* before it was itself accepted (first in 1959). To philistines *Lady Chatterley's Lover* may have seemed the more dangerous of the two books. Joyce, however filthy his expressions, was after all only reflecting life, and with graphic accuracy, but Lawrence was doing something more. If Joyce's book was in any way philosophical, it was artistically so in that its detailed realism represented a certain approach to art. Its philosophy of life is eternally arguable, depending for example on whether Molly Bloom's triple affirmation at the end of the book is really yea-saying to life. But the intention of *Lady Chatterley* is beyond argument: Lawrence was certainly yea-saying. He disliked Flaubert and Tolstoy, in their different ways, almost as much as he disliked Joyce, and often said so. Tolstoy's Anna Karenina had betrayed the marriage agreement, and so had Flaubert's Emma Bovary: both these authors sent their heroines to death by suicide. Lawrence on the contrary led Connie Chatterley towards life. He didn't feel, in her case, that the love affair outside marriage was 'immoral'. And he was not advocating adultery, even in terms of an Oliver Mellors: 'Far be it from me to recommend that all women should be running after gamekeepers for lovers', Lawrence wrote in *A Propos of Lady Chatterley's Lover*. He admitted that Connie would lose the sympathy of some readers because Clifford was crippled, but the character of Clifford had come to Lawrence that way and he let the condition stand. The story would of course have been better if Clifford had merely been intellectually sexual, like Michaelis, a representative of what Lawrence called the counterfeit.

Lawrence and Frieda at
Villa Mirenda

But the story has many fine Lawrencean touches. As so often in his fiction, he makes use of the sleeping-beauty or briar-rose princess theme: Connie is dreaming her way through life, and Mellors breaks through the thorns (they are very real thorns) to release her. There is also the ritual of the baptismal rain through which Connie and Mellors run naked in the woodland. As for symbols, the house in which the Chatterleys live, Wragby, is hell itself, filled with sulphur fumes from the nearby mines. Connie, walking through the wood in which Mellors lives, thinks of herself as Persephone 'out of hell on a cold morning'—Persephone who in the vegetation-myth of the Eleusinian mysteries of the Greeks stands for the renewal of life, the flourishing of the crops in the seasons when she is allowed to leave hell. And, in Lawrence's novel, Mellors will take Connie away from hell for ever.

Fresco from the Tomb of the Leopards, Tarquinia. 'And so they move on, on their long, sandalled feet, past the little berried olive-trees, swiftly going with their limbs full of life, full of life to the tips. This sense of vigorous, strong-bodied liveliness is characteristic of the Etruscans, and is somehow beyond art.' *(Etruscan Places)*

'Etruscan Places'   In the spring of 1927, while still working on this book, Lawrence made a tour with Earl Brewster of the Etruscan tombs and ruined cities along the western (Maremma) coast of central Italy. Lawrence wrote a series of essays (published after his death as *Etruscan Places*, 1932) in which he expressed his admiration for a 'blood-knowledge' culture which the brutal and machine-like Romans had destroyed. Soon after he returned to Florence, he had to show two American women about the city, and he wrote to Brewster about this: 'They simply *can't see* anything: you might as well ask a dog to look at a picture or a statue.'

Aldous Huxley. '... the Aldous that writes those novels is only one little Aldous amongst others—probably much nicer—that don't write novels.... I don't like his books: even if I admire a sort of desperate courage of repulsion and repudiation in them. But again, I feel that only half a man writes the books—a sort of precocious adolescent.' (Letter)

The Huxleys

Aldous Huxley and his wife Maria were occasional visitors at Villa Mirenda, and the Lawrences liked them, even if Lawrence cared little for Huxley's clever novels. Huxley was in Lawrence's view over-intellectualized (as Lawrence himself of course was, and this is one reason he fought against the condition in others); but Huxley paid him serious, open-minded attention when they argued about science, which to Lawrence had become one of the great menaces of the world.

Les Diablerets, Switzerland, where the Lawrences stayed from January to March 1928. '... we came up here to see if it would do me good—the altitude—only about 3,500, but fairly high for Europe—and the snow and the sun.' (Letter)

Switzerland   In January 1928, while at Les Diablerets, Switzerland, Lawrence received a visit of homage from an articulate member of the young generation, Rolf Gardiner, whose ambition (later realized) was to revive ancient English customs and ceremonials. Another visitor, whom the Lawrences later stayed with in Bavaria, was the German physician and playwright, Max Mohr.

In June 1928, the Lawrences left Villa Mirenda forever, and went to Switzerland with the Brewsters, spending the last part of the summer in a chalet at Gsteig bei Gstaad, not yet a famous resort. Lawrence was intermittently very ill, but the attempt to arrange for subscribers to receive their smuggled copies of *Lady Chatterley* in different parts of the world gave him surges of energy. Yet he

Maria Huxley

was also capable at this time of detachment; just before going to Gsteig he wrote, at Chexbres-sur-Vevey, his charming little essay on *Insouciance,* later collected in *Assorted Articles* (1930). In it he expressed a wish that a little English woman at his hotel wouldn't 'care' so much about everything. And Lawrence's last notable work of fiction emphasizes such a withdrawal. This book was *The Escaped Cock* (1929; also known as *The Man Who Died*). The story takes place in a colony of the Roman world, and concerns a prophet who has been crucified and who, after his resurrection, gives up his prophesying, to find fulfilment in love with a virgin priestess of Isis.

Lawrence painted at Gsteig: when Maria Huxley had brought some canvases to the Villa Mirenda he had taken up that activity again, this time not copying, as in his youth, but painting landscapes and portraits, often mingling religion with eroticism.

Lawrence and his sister Emily at Gsteig bei Gstaad. '... we have Emily and her daughter—and it is really rather suffering—and Emily, poor Emily, she can't help feeling that ninepence is exactly half as good again as sixpence. If I wearily protest that ninepence is nothing to me unless it's ninepence-worth of life, she just looks at me as if I'd said nothing.' (Letter)

Brigit Patmore and Richard Aldington near St Tropez. '... the Aldingtons are old friends. So is Brigit Patmore. We get on very well, and I'm the only disagreeable one.' (Letter)

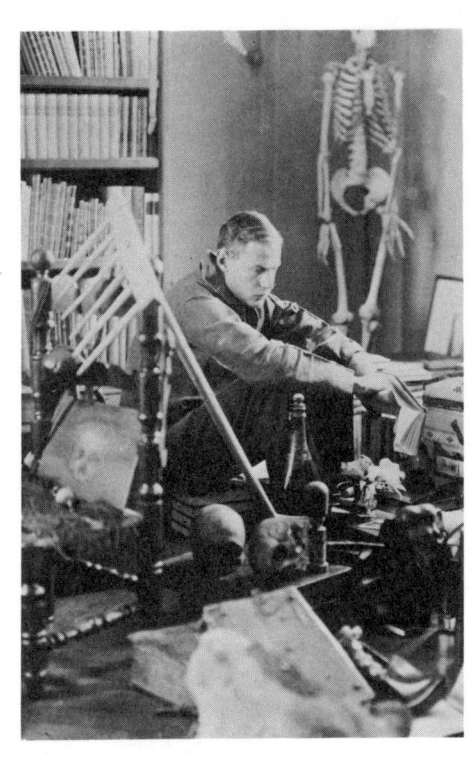

Harry Crosby, Paris 1928. '... Harry has a real poetic gift ...' (Letter)

Caresse Crosby, photographed by Lawrence at Le Moulin du Soleil in 1929

Richard Aldington had been given the use of a *vigie,* or fortress, off the French coast below Toulon, and had invited the Lawrences and several other friends, including Brigit Patmore and Dorothy Yorke, to stay with him there. Lawrence, sick and bitter, found fault with the novel Aldington was writing, *Death of a Hero,* and with the one Huxley had just published, *Point Counter Point,* whose portrait of Lawrence as Mark Rampion was supposed to be flattering, though the original of the character heartily disliked it.

By mid-November, Lawrence and Frieda had settled for the winter at a hotel in Bandol, on the French coast; by mid-March they were at Paris. There they met the exciting Harry and Caresse Crosby, new American friends whose Black Sun Press first published *The Escaped Cock* and other work by Lawrence. In April he and Frieda went to Spain, where they stayed until mid-June.

Lawrence at
Le Moulin du Soleil

Lawrence's paintings Lawrence then travelled to visit Orioli in Florence, while Frieda went to see the exhibition of her husband's pictures at the Warren Gallery in London. The richly coloured paintings attracted the scorn of some of the critics and the attention of Scotland Yard: policemen removed thirteen of the pictures. A police magistrate threatened to have them burned, but let Frieda's solicitor take them upon assurance that they would not be exhibited again in England. The book of coloured reproductions, *The Paintings of D. H. Lawrence,* was suppressed, but a new and different version of it appeared in 1964, published openly in Britain and America.

Exhibition of Lawrence's paintings at the Warren Gallery, Maddox Street, in 1929

Dorothy Warren and her husband,
Philip Trotter, owners of
the Warren Gallery

The latter volume presents in colour only those paintings by Lawrence from the Warren Gallery exhibition of which the originals could be traced for new reproductions, but all the rest of those pictures appear without colour. A number of other paintings by Lawrence are also included in the book, some in colour; most of these were made in Lawrence's youth, when he frequently copied the work of well-known artists. He had not formally studied painting, though he had a few lessons in drawing; but he gave a great deal of attention to the copies he made. It was not until 1926, however, that he began painting in earnest, producing original work. His pictures took second place to his writing, yet when he learned that the London magistrate might order them to be burned, he wrote to tell Dorothy Warren that he didn't 'under any circumstances, or for any cause' want his paintings destroyed. He was willing to do his bit to help the cause of English liberty, but 'to admit that my pictures should be burned, in order to change an English law, would be to admit that sacrifice of life to circumstance which I most strongly disbelieve in.' He would not be a martyr.

Fortunately the paintings were released, and for a number of years after Lawrence's death in 1930 they were at Martha Gordon Crotch's Pottery Shop in Vence, in southern France, the town in which he died. Frieda later brought most of them to New Mexico, but unfortunately the whereabouts of some of them are unknown, and at least one of them—*North Sea*—was finally burned (in the fire that destroyed Aldous Huxley's California home in 1961). From the two volumes of the paintings—that is, the books of 1929 and 1964—and from the eight paintings on permanent exhibition at Saki Karavas's La Fonda Hotel in Taos and the three located at the Humanities Research Center of the University of Texas, it is possible to make some statements about Lawrence as a painter. Painters and art critics who see his work usually have quite different views about it. Some say that Lawrence had great natural gifts and, with training and long practice, might have become a fine painter; others think that he had no true gift and would have remained an amateur.

A letter Lawrence sent to Harry Crosby before leaving for Spain

Lawrence at Palma de Mallorca, Spain, 1929

Perhaps his best painting is one of those now in Texas: *Boccaccio Story*. This canvas has a living quality, with Lawrence's rich colouring; and it presents a dramatic human picture (the gardener, sexually exposed, lying asleep, and the startled nuns discovering him): the positions of the gardener's legs and arms form balanced angles, the nuns appear in juxtaposition to two white dogs on the opposite side of the picture, and the furrows of earth running in somewhat different directions in the centre and background of the painting give it a rhythmic quality. This is heightened by the rows of delicately coloured, plumy trees in the background. There is an almost equally fine effect in *Red Willow Trees* in the Karavas collection: three naked men in the foreground bathe in a stream that winds among hills and vermilion willow trees, with a slope full of umbrella pines beyond. Again the composition has balance and wonderful colour. Many of the paintings, however, are fairly crude—Lawrence was particularly bad at drawing arms—but most of them strike the attention forcibly, and the colouring is often as rich as in Lawrence's poetry and prose.

Two of Lawrence's paintings: *Boccaccio Story (above)* and *Red Willow Trees (below)*

Villa Beau Soleil, Bandol. 'It is on the sea—rather lovely—a smallish bungalow, six rooms, terrace—bath, central heating—some neglected garden . . . . It is ordinary, but poky—and wonderfully in the air and light.' (Letter)

He is not a major painter as he is a major writer, yet his pictures are full of vitality and delight. They cannot be ignored in any serious consideration of Lawrence. As Sir Herbert Read has said, 'Indeed, one must now conclude that any complete understanding of Lawrence as a writer is not possible unless one takes into account his work as a painter.'

Late work Lawrence, infuriated by the seizure of the pictures and the bowdlerization of his book of poems, *Pansies* (1929), became desperately ill in Florence. In July Frieda brought him to Baden-Baden for a rest, and in September they returned to Bandol, where they rented the Villa Beau Soleil. En route they had stopped in Bavaria, where Lawrence wrote one of his greatest poems, *Bavarian Gentians*:

let me guide myself with the blue, forked torch of this flower
down the darker and darker stairs, where blue is darkened on blueness.

He knew that he was near death, which he had held off for so long, to the astonishment of doctors. He allowed one to examine him in Bavaria because the man was also a poet—Hans Carossa—who was amazed that Lawrence could go on living.

A view of Vence. 'Here one is in the sky again, and on top of things.' (Letter)

Lawrence also wrote poems at Bandol, as he looked out on the bright sea and saw ancient pagans sailing upon it, golden Hellenes who were more living than the coastal steamers with their trails of dirty smoke.

Meanwhile, in England, Lawrence's pamphlet *Pornography and Obscenity* was having a brisk sale. It was soon to be followed by a little book that presented one of his finest essays, *A Propos of Lady Chatterley's Lover* (1930). Lawrence on his sunlit coast wrote another remarkable poem, *The Ship of Death*:

> *Oh build your ship of death. Oh build it!*
> *for you will need it*
> *For the voyage of oblivion awaits you.*

And he wrote one more prose piece long enough to be made into a book after his death: *Apocalypse* (1931), his last religious utterance, and his last hymn to the sun. The essay grew out of his interest in the Book of Revelation, stimulated by the English artist and mystic, Frederick Carter.

Ad Astra sanatorium, Vence. '. . . I have a balcony and see the coast-line and Cannes five miles off.' (Letter)

By 6 February Lawrence was for the first time ill enough to move to a sanatorium. His London friend, the painter Mark Gertler, recommended the specialist Dr Andrew Morland, who in turn recommended the sanatorium: the Ad Astra at Vence, in the hills above Nice. Frieda lived at a nearby hotel. Lawrence's visitors included the Aga Khan, H. G. Wells, and the Huxleys; the American sculptor Jo Davidson made a bust of him. From his balcony Lawrence could see the mimosas and the almond blossoming; but he was burning away in his illness.

Death   On 1 March Lawrence left the sanatorium for the Villa Robermond, now the Villa Aurella, in Vence. A doctor came to give him a morphine injection. Frieda remembered, 'I held his ankle from time to time, it felt so full of life, all my days I shall hold his ankle in my hand.' On the night of 2 March 1930, at ten o'clock, Lawrence died. He was buried in the local cemetery until, in 1935, Angelo Ravagli went to Vence and had his remains cremated. He brought the ashes to America, where they rest in a tomb at Kiowa ranch. Frieda is now buried in front of the tomb, which looks down the mountainside to the Rio Grande; it has become a place to which literary pilgrimages are made.

'Jo Davidson came and made a clay head of me—made me tired. . . . ' (Letter)

(Left) Villa Robermond (now Villa Aurella), where Lawrence died 2 March 1930. 'Oh build your ship of death . . . Oh, nothing matters but the longest journey.' *(Ship of Death)*

(Below) Lawrence's grave at Vence 1930-35

(Right) Lawrence's tomb at Kiowa ranch, summer 1954, before the addition of Frieda's gravestone

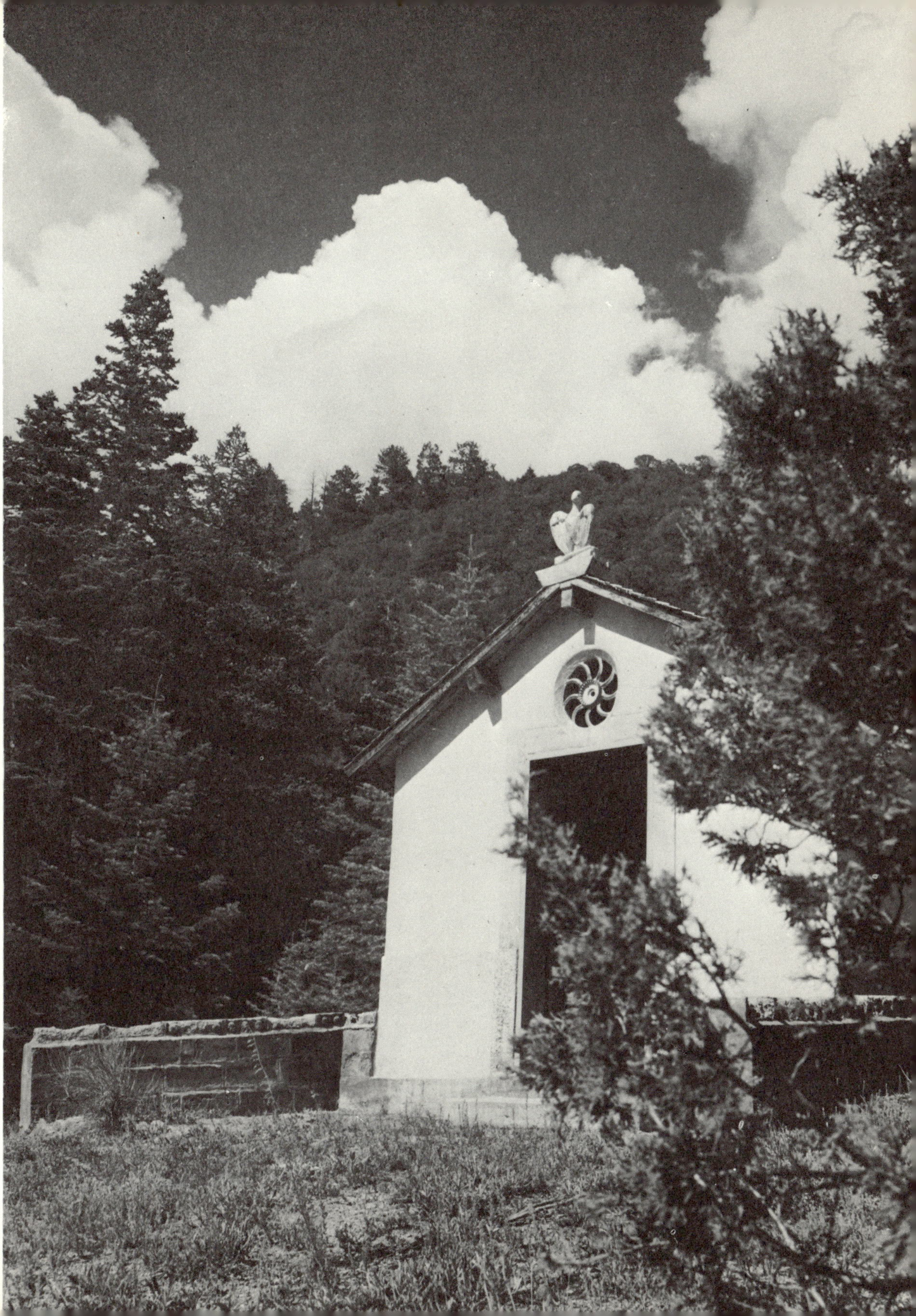

The tomb at Kiowa: exterior *(left)*, interior *(below left)*. The cross of Frieda's grave can be seen immediately outside the tomb

The Lawrence family grave at Eastwood

BIBLIOGRAPHICAL NOTES

Lawrence, a controversial figure for most of his life, became the cause of even greater contention as soon as he died. Many of the obituary notices were downright vicious. A particularly nasty one appeared in *The New Yorker,* written by Genêt (Janet Flanner), who reported that Lawrence 'had, among other eccentricities, a fancy for removing his clothes and climbing mulberry trees'—only one of the many *canards* about Lawrence. T. S. Eliot, Clive Bell, and J. C. Squire were among others who wrote denigratingly of Lawrence, but their statements dealt with his work rather than the supposed 'eccentricities' of the man. Lawrence was, however, staunchly defended in the press by such old friends as Catherine Carswell. Lady Ottoline Morrell, who had forgiven Lawrence for portraying her as Hermione in *Women in Love,* spoke up for him in a public letter signed by her initials; Murry was anonymous in his defence of Lawrence. E. M. Forster, under his own name, wrote of him with generosity and appreciation.

Almost immediately afterwards, volumes of memoirs began to appear, most of them presenting a debased portrait of Lawrence. Two exceptions were Richard Aldington's *D. H. Lawrence* (1930), a reprint of a pamphlet of three years earlier, which had mildly amused Lawrence, and Rebecca West's *Elegy* (1930), taken from a magazine article that appeared soon after Lawrence's death. Rebecca West said that she had first heard that Lawrence was gravely ill while she was attending a performance of the dramatization of Huxley's *Point Counter Point* (as *This Way to Paradise*). She immediately thought what a loss to the play it would have been if the character representing Lawrence (Mark Rampion) had been omitted: 'Even so did those of us who heard of Lawrence's death feel that from the spectacle of the universe, by the incredible stupidity of a destroying angel, the best thing had gone.' Stephen Potter's little book, *D. H. Lawrence: A First Study* (1930), was a purely critical exposition of the writings, almost entirely favourable. Then came Murry's *Son of Woman* (1931), which Aldous Huxley spoke of as a 'curious essay in destructive hagiology'. Murry was one of the leading British critics of this century, but *Son of Woman* was a mistake, though he partly rectified it in 1957, the year of his death, in *Love, Freedom and Society: An Analytic Comparison of D. H. Lawrence and Albert Schweitzer.* Murry was usually better when writing about authors of the past, whom he didn't know; as Lawrence once pointed out to Murry, he had overestimated his wife Katherine Mansfield; and he was later to underestimate Lawrence himself in *Son of Woman,* which is partly a denigration of the man and partly a denigration of his work. It was a time when the psychoanalytical approach to biography was popular. Murry at least showed a certain originality in drawing less upon Freud than upon Adler in his misunderstanding of Lawrence. But the years improved Murry's vision, and eventually he wrote of him more sensibly.

Young Lorenzo: Early Life of D. H. Lawrence (1932), by Lawrence's sister Ada (Mrs W. E. Clarke) and a Nottingham journalist, G. Stuart Gelder, was a sympathetic picture of the author's youth. But Mabel Dodge Luhan's *Lorenzo in Taos* (1932) showed Lawrence through the eyes of a neurotic woman. Her book and Murry's did enormous damage to his literary reputation. Readers of such volumes as Mrs Luhan's would hardly be convinced that the Lawrence they showed could have written anything worth reading, and the damage was not undone by two friendlier volumes of reminiscence, Catherine Carswell's *The Savage Pilgrimage* (1932) and the Hon. Dorothy Brett's *Lawrence and Brett* (1933). Murry's *Reminiscences of D. H. Lawrence* (1933) was both a reprint of his memoirs of his former friend, which had appeared serially in *The*

Bibliographical Notes

Adelphi, and an answer to Mrs Carswell's book, which had attacked Murry. Because he threatened to bring an action, Mrs Carswell's publishers had to withdraw her book and reprint one page. He had objected to Mrs Carswell's statement about Lawrence's irritation when he returned from America in 1923 to find that Murry and Frieda had been 'chummy' in London; Murry had told Lawrence that he wanted him to take over *The Adelphi* and was merely acting as his lieutenant, *locum tenens*, until Lawrence should arrive; Mrs Carswell commented, 'though Murry might be Lawrence's self-appointed lieutenant on *The Adelphi*, Frieda was another matter ... In Lawrence's marriage there was no place for any kind of lieutenancy.'

The reason for Murry's suit to have the book withdrawn may now be told: with the publication of parts of Murry's journal after his death, readers learned that Frieda had suggested to him that they become lovers, an idea he had rejected because of loyalty to Lawrence; in the light of this knowledge his threatened action against the publishers no longer seems unreasonable. But Mrs Carswell's cause seemed a noble one at the time, and Murry's *Son of Woman* had certainly helped to reduce Lawrence's stature as a writer. Even perceptive critical volumes such as Anaïs Nin's *D. H. Lawrence: A Critical Study* (1932) could not at that time remedy this (fortunately Miss Nin's book was reprinted in 1964). Lawrence's *Letters* (1932), edited by Aldous Huxley, indicated to a good many readers that Lawrence was a first-rate writer, and sent them back to his imaginative works; but still his reputation did not increase perceptibly. One reason for this was the world-wide depression and later the world-wide war. People became interested in reading about socio-political matters, and turned their attention to novelists of other kinds, little realizing that Lawrence had made profound socio-political comments or that he had written of the modern world as a prophet and with more vital insights than most other authors. This was not widely recognized until after the Second World War, when the Lawrence revival began.

Meanwhile, the biographies had continued to appear in the 1930s. *D. H. Lawrence: Reminiscences and Correspondence* (1934), by E. and A. Brewster, was a sensible and detached book, but it apparently made little impression. Frieda's vigorous biography, *Not I, But the Wind* (1934), plangently defended Lawrence, but still his books remained unread. Jessie Chambers (writing under the initials E. T.) showed in *D. H. Lawrence: A Personal Record* (1935) how cruelly the friend of her youth had treated her, and she indulged in some self-justification, incidentally revealing how little she really understood the man she had futilely loved. When the collection of Lawrence's writings, *Phoenix*, appeared in 1936, Clifton Fadiman in *The New Yorker* was publicly amused that such a writer could have attracted so much attention in the 1920s; an appraisal in *The Nation* (New York) by Harry T. Moore said that *Phoenix* would be 'an influential book', and indeed it has proved to be so. In 1938, another of the more sympathetic memoirs appeared, *A Poet and Two Painters*, by the Danish artist Knud Merrild, who tried to make a book-length reminiscence by muddling together a number of Lawrence's printed statements and disguising them as conversation. Hugh Kingsmill's *D. H. Lawrence* (1938) muddled together all the memoirs in a way that made Lawrence look more ridiculous than most of the individual memoirs had done. William York Tindall's *D. H. Lawrence and Susan His Cow* (1939) used Lawrence's own writings in order to ridicule him, but was an important book because it applied genuine scholarship to the subject, particularly in its examination of sources for *The Plumed Serpent*. By this time, however, readers had become tired of Lawrence even as an object of mockery, and with the coming of the second war he slid into almost total oblivion. Yet it was Professor Tindall who helped pave the way for a revaluation of Lawrence when, in *Forces in Modern British Literature* (1946), he courageously indicated in public a change of mind and said in effect that, since we all now faced the possibility of being blown up, Lawrence's prophecies no longer sounded quite so foolish.

The revival began. Richard Aldington's *Portrait of a Genius, But...* (1950) lamented that people had always said 'Of course Lawrence is a genius, but...'; and if Aldington was sometimes amusing at Lawrence's expense, he was also basically sympathetic. And now a generation of writers who had not known Lawrence personally began to deal with him, usually with detachment: Anthony West in *D. H. Lawrence* (1950), Harry T. Moore in *The Life and Works of D. H. Lawrence* (1951) and *The Intelligent Heart* (1955), Father William Tiverton (Martin Jarrett-Kerr) in *D. H. Lawrence and Human Existence* (1951), F. R. Leavis in *D. H. Lawrence: Novelist* (1955), and Mark Spilka in *The Love Ethic of D. H. Lawrence* (1955). One last unfriendly memoir came out in 1951, Witter Bynner's *Journey With Genius*. In *D. H. Lawrence: A Composite Biography* (1957-9), Edward Nehls usefully brought together a number of the memoirs in perspective and added various new ones, in a three-volume work of the highest value to students of modern literature.

The *D. H. Lawrence News and Notes* is a lively, witty little newsletter, edited now and then by Dexter Martin from the State University of California. Lawrence books of all kinds continue to appear. In 1962, Armin Arnold usefully collected the earlier version of Lawrence's American-literature essays as *The Symbolic Meaning*. Also in 1962, the two-volume edition of Lawrence's *Collected Letters* came out. In 1963, Warren Robert's *A Bibliography of D. H. Lawrence* supplanted earlier volumes by Edward D. McDonald (1925 and 1931) and by E. W. Tedlock, Jr (1948) Of recent critical studies, *D. H. Lawrence: The Failure and Triumph of Art.* (1960), by Eliseo Vivas, is the most seasoned, although interesting volumes appeared in 1963 by Eugene Goodheart (*The Utopian Vision of D. H. Lawrence*), Julian Moynihan (*The Deed of Life*), Daniel Weiss (*Oedipus in Nottingham*), and Kingsley Widmer (*The Art of Perversity*); E. W. Tedlock, Jr's *D. H. Lawrence: Artist and Rebel* (1964) demonstrates that Lawrence's vitalism outweighs his tendencies towards nihilism. Ronald Draper's *D. H. Lawrence* (1964) and George H. Ford's *Double Measure: A Study of the Novels and Stories of D. H. Lawrence* (1965) add importantly to the criticism of this outstanding novelist and poet, whose *Complete Poems* were published in 1964, edited by V. de Sola Pinto and Warren Roberts.

Bibliographical Notes

CHRONOLOGY

1885 Lawrence born at Eastwood, Nottinghamshire on 11 September, the fourth of the five children of a collier married to an ex-schoolteacher.

1893-8 Attends Beauvale Board School; he is a delicate child who spends most of his time with the girls.

1898- Having won a county council scholarship, Lawrence studies at Nottingham
1901 High School.

1901 Meets Jessie Chambers; she and Lawrence become close companions, forming a relationship finally severed only in 1912. Lawrence becomes a clerk in an artificial-limbs factory in Nottingham.

1901-2 Winter: Lawrence's mother nurses him through a severe attack of pneumonia; this increases his emotional dependence on her.

1902 Lawrence becomes a teacher at the British School, Eastwood.

1903 Becomes a pupil-teacher at nearby Ilkeston, Derbyshire, where he meets Louise Burrows; they are friends for about eight years.

1904 December: comes first in all England and Wales in the King's Scholarship Examination.

1905 Teaches at the British School, Eastwood in order to be able to afford to go to college.

1906 Lawrence begins writing his first novel, *The White Peacock*. September: begins two-year course for the teacher's certificate at Nottingham University College.

1908 Lawrence becomes a teacher at the Davidson Road School, Croydon; away from his mother's influence he becomes engaged to a fellow-teacher, Agnes Holt and begins an intimate friendship with another teacher, Helen Corke.

1909 November: some poems—the first of Lawrence's works to be seriously published—appear in *The English Review*.

1910 December: Lawrence's mother dies.

1911 January: *The White Peacock* published. December: start of the severe illness that drives Lawrence away from teaching.

1912 April: meets Mrs Frieda Weekley (born von Richthofen). May: Lawrence and Frieda go to Metz, where Lawrence is arrested as a spy. They take a house at Icking, near Munich, where Lawrence writes most of the cycle of poems *Look! We Have Come Through!* Publication of Lawrence's second novel, *The Trespasser*, based on Helen Corke's experiences. Lawrence and Frieda move to Gargnano, Lago di Garda.

1913 February: appearance of Lawrence's *Love Poems*. May: *Sons and Lovers* published. June: Lawrence and Frieda return to England, form an important relationship with Middleton Murry and

Chronology

Katherine Mansfield, and meet Herbert and Cynthia Asquith. September: they go to Fiascherino, Italy. Lawrence works on what was to become the two novels *The Rainbow* and *Women in Love*.

1914 Frieda's divorce comes through: she and Lawrence return to London in June and are married in July.

1915 Lawrence becomes for a time a close friend of Bertrand Russell. *The Rainbow* published (September) and legally declared obscene (November). Lawrence and Frieda move to Cornwall at the end of the year.

1916 Lawrence completes *Women in Love*. He and Frieda are officially and unofficially persecuted because of their attitude to the war and because of Frieda's German birth. Lawrence's poems *Amores* appear; also his travel book, *Twilight in Italy*.

1917 *Look! We Have Come Through!* published. Persecution culminates in October, when Lawrence and Frieda are ordered to leave Cornwall, to stay away from the coast, and to report regularly to the police. Lawrence for the second time rejected as unfit for the army because of his weak chest. Starts writing *Studies in Classic American Literature* (published 1923).

1919 November: Lawrence and Frieda go to Italy, settling at Capri.

1920 *Women in Love* published in the U.S.A. March: Lawrence and Frieda move to Taormina, Sicily, where Lawrence writes many of the poems of *Birds, Beasts and Flowers* (published 1923).

1921 Lawrence finishes *Aaron's Rod* (published 1922). *Women in Love* published in London. Also travel book, *Sea and Sardinia*.

1922 February: Lawrence and Frieda leave Sicily for Ceylon. May: they arrive in Australia, stay at Thirroul, New South Wales, where Lawrence writes *Kangaroo* (published 1923). September: they arrive at Taos, New Mexico, as the guests of Mrs Mabel Dodge Sterne (later Luhan), but in December move to the nearby Del Monte ranch.

1923 Lawrence and Frieda stay in Mexico City, then move to Chapala, where Lawrence begins *The Plumed Serpent*. After they go to New York, their relationship deteriorates, and Frieda returns to England (August), Lawrence crossing in November.

1924 March: Lawrence and Frieda return to New and Old Mexico with the painter Dorothy Brett, the only one of Lawrence's friends willing to help him found his utopian colony, Rananim. The Lawrences move to Kiowa ranch.

1925 January: Brett leaves the Lawrences at Frieda's insistence. Lawrence finishes *The Plumed Serpent* (published 1926) and becomes terribly ill with what was apparently the beginning of his tuberculosis. September: after returning to New Mexico, he and Frieda leave America and settle at Spotorno, on the Italian Riviera.

1926 May: Lawrence and Frieda move to the Villa Mirenda, outside Florence. Lawrence begins painting seriously.

1927 Travel book, *Mornings in Mexico*.

1928 Lawrence completes *Lady Chatterley's Lover* at the Mirenda; it is privately printed in Florence. He and Frieda move to Bandol, southern France.

1929 June: Lawrence's paintings exhibited in

Chronology

London. July: thirteen of the pictures are removed by the police; and Lawrence's solicitor prevents their destruction by promising that they will not be exhibited again in England. The book *The Paintings of D. H. Lawrence* suppressed. A number of poems have to be excluded from the collection *Pansies*, although Lawrence issues a complete edition, privately printed. He now becomes gravely ill.

1930　Lawrence dies at Vence on 2 March.

1932　*The Letters of D. H. Lawrence* appear. Also *Etruscan Places*.

1935　Lawrence's body is cremated and his ashes brought to a mountainside tomb above Kiowa ranch.

1959　First unexpurgated edition of *Lady Chatterley* published in the U.S.A.; the British edition appears in the following year. In both cases there is an unsuccessful prosecution for obscenity.

1962　Publication of *The Collected Letters of D. H. Lawrence*.

1964　A new edition of *The Paintings of D. H. Lawrence* published in Britain and America, also his *Complete Poems*.

NOTES ON THE PICTURES

Frontispiece. D. H. LAWRENCE, 4 November 1924. *Photo Edward Weston*

5 BRINSLEY COLLIERY where Lawence's father worked. *Photo H. T. Moore*

6 LAWRENCE'S BIRTHPLACE. Lawrence's mother had to give up the shop on the ground floor as her family increased. *Photo Nottingham Public Library*
LONG ROW, Nottingham. *Photo lent by George Lazarus*
NOTTINGHAM ROAD, Eastwood. *Photo lent by George Lazarus*

7 THE LAWRENCE FAMILY. *Photo lent by H. T. Moore*

8 ALBERT STREET CONGREGATIONAL CHAPEL, Eastwood, where the Lawrence family worshipped. Adjoining the Sunday school was the British School where Lawrence first taught 1905-6. *Photo Warren Roberts*

9 LAWRENCE with some classmates at Beauvale Board School. *Photo D. H. Lawrence Collection, The University of Texas*
BEAUVALE BOARD SCHOOL, Eastwood, where Lawrence was a pupil 1893-98. *Photo Nottingham Public Library*
NOTTINGHAM HIGH SCHOOL. *Photo Warren Roberts*

10 MOORGREEN COLLIERY, near Eastwood, *Photo lent by H. T. Moore*

11 VIEW FROM FELLEY MILL (Strelley Mill in *The White Peacock*) showing the Haggs (Willey Farm in *Sons and Lovers*). *Photo Nottingham Public Library*

12 BRITISH SCHOOL, Albert Street, Eastwood. *Photo Nottingham Public Library*
THE BREACH, Eastwood. *Photo Nottingham Public Library*

13 MOORGREEN RESERVOIR (Nethermere in *The White Peacock* and Willey Water in *Women in Love*). *Photo Nottingham Public Library*

14 LAMB CLOSE HOUSE, Moorgreen (the Highclose of *The White Peacock*, the Shortlands of *Women in Love* and the Wragby of *Lady Chatterley's Lover*). *Photo Warren Roberts*

15 THE MISK HILLS, and the road to Haggs Farm. *Photo Nottingham Public Library*

16 HAGGS FARM, Underwood. *Photo Nottingham Public Library*

17 JESSIE CHAMBERS (later Mrs John R. Wood) *c.* 1905. *Photo lent by H. T. Moore*

18 UNIVERSITY COLLEGE, Shakespeare Street, Nottingham. Now the city's public library. *Photo Nottingham Public Library*

19 LAWRENCE, 11 September 1906. *Photo lent by H. T. Moore*

20 DAVIDSON ROAD SCHOOL, Croydon. *Photo Warren Roberts*
HELEN CORKE *c.* 1912. *Photo lent by Helen Corke*

21 FELLEY MILL POND (Strelley Mill of *The White Peacock*). *Photo Warren Roberts*

22 LAWRENCE'S MOTHER in the back garden

135

Notes of the Lynn Croft house in 1910. *Photo lent by H. T. Moore*

EDWARD GARNETT c. 1911. *Photo lent by David Garnett*

23 FELLEY MILL POND. *Photo Nottingham Public Library*

24 THE MISK HILLS and the road to Haggs Farm. *Photo Nottingham Public Library*

25 FELLEY MILL FARM. *Photo Nottingham Public Library*

26 COWLEY, Victoria Crescent, Mapperley. *Photo Nottingham Public Library*

27 FRIEDA WEEKLEY. *Photo lent by Montague Weekley*

28 FRIEDA with Ernest Weekley and his parents. *Photo D. H. Lawrence Collection, The University of Texas*
FRIEDA with her son, Montague, 1901. *Photo lent by Montague Weekley*
FRIEDA with Ernest Weekley in Germany. *Photo lent by Montague Weekley*

29 BARONESS VON RICHTHOFEN. *Photo D. H. Lawrence Collection, The University of Texas*
BARON FRIEDRICH VON RICHTHOFEN. *Photo lent by Montague Weekley*

30 THE RIVER SIEG AT HENNEF. *Photo R. F. Amity*

31 THE HOUSE AT ICKING (owned by Alfred Weber) in which the Lawrences stayed in 1912. *Photo H. T. Moore*

32 LAWRENCE c. 1912. *Photo lent by H. T. Moore*

33 LAGO DI GARDA, Italy. Gargnano is on the western shore. *Photo M. Hürlimann*

34 SAN TOMMASO, Gargnano. *Photo H. T. Moore*
VILLA IGÉA, Gargnano, where the Lawrences lived from 1912 to 1913. *Photo H. T. Moore*

35 DAVID GARNETT, drawn by Lawrence in June 1913 at The Cearne, the Garnett's house in Kent. *By courtesy of David Garnett*

36 DAVID GARNETT. *Photo Mansell Collection*

37 JACKET DESIGN for *Sons and Lovers*, possibly by Ernest Collings. D. H. Lawrence Collection, The University of Texas.

38 CASTLE GATE BUILDINGS, Nottingham. The premises of J. H. Haywood Ltd (the Thomas Jordan & Co. of *Sons and Lovers*) are through the archway near the street-lamp. Lawrence worked here briefly as a clerk in 1901. *Photo Nottingham Public Library*

39 NOTTINGHAM CASTLE, where Paul exhibits his paintings in *Sons and Lovers*. *Photo lent by H. T. Moore*

40 KATHERINE MANSFIELD (born Kathleen Beauchamp), a writer from New Zealand who married the English critic John Middleton Murry. *Photo Radio Times Hulton Picture Library*

41 LAWRENCE, Katherine Mansfield, Frieda and Murry in Kensington 1915. *Photo lent by H. T. Moore*

42 BROADSTAIRS, Kent. Early nineteenth-century print. *Photo Thames and Hudson Archives*

43 LADY CYNTHIA ASQUITH (born Cynthia Charteris), wife of the Hon. Herbert Asquith. *Photo Bassano and Vandyk Studios*

Notes

44 VILLINO ETTORE GAMBROSIER, Fiascherino, Italy, where the Lawrences stayed 1913-14. *Photo lent by Leo Hamalian*

45 CATHERINE CARSWELL *c.* 1910. *Photo lent by John Carswell*

46 VIOLA MEYNELL. *Photo The Mansell Collection*

47 SHED HALL, Greatham, which Lawrence used as the setting for *England, My England*. *Photo lent by Dr Mary Saleeby Fisher*

48 LADY OTTOLINE MORRELL at Garsington Manor, Oxfordshire 1916. *By courtesy of Mrs Igor Vinogradoff*
LAWRENCE, Philip Heseltine and Dikrān Kouyoudjian at Garsington *c.* 1915. *By courtesy of Mrs Igor Vinogradoff*

49 A PORTRAIT OF LAWRENCE reproduced in *T.P.'s and Cassell's Weekly*, 18 July 1925. *Photo Nottingham Public Library*

50 1 BYRON VILLAS, Hampstead. *Photo Peter Coviello*

51 LAWRENCE'S DRAWING OF EASTWOOD, made on the day he finished *The Rainbow*, and given to Viola Meynell. *Photo lent by H. T. Moore*

52 'THE NEW STATESMAN'S report of the difficulties over *The Rainbow*. *Photo Thames and Hudson Archives*

53 THE ORIGINAL OF MARSH FARM in *The Rainbow*, near Cossall (Cossethay in the novel), Derbyshire. *Photo H. T. Moore*
CHURCH COTTAGE, Cossall. *Photo Warren Roberts*

54 CHURCH COTTAGE, Cossall. *Photo Nottingham Public Library*

55 MINNIE LUCIE CHANNING, the Pussum or Minette of *Women in Love*. *Photo lent by Boris de Croustchoff*

56 LAWRENCE'S COTTAGE at Higher Tregerthen, Zennor (1916-17). *Photo Thames and Hudson Archives*

57 SIR THOMAS PHILIP BARBER provided Lawrence with some of the external features for Gerald Crich in *Women in Love*. *Photo lent by H. T. Moore*

58 SOUTHWELL MINSTER, Nottinghamshire. The town was visited by Rupert Birkin and Ursula Brangwen in *Women in Love*. *Photo lent by George Lazarus*

59 JOHN MIDDLETON MURRY *c.* 1916. *Photo lent by H. T. Moore*

60 HILDA DOOLITTLE (H.D.), the American poet and wife of Richard Aldington *c.* 1949. *Photo Associated Press*

61 MOUNTAIN COTTAGE, Middleton-by-Wirksworth, Derbyshire, where the Lawrences lived intermittently from 1918 to 1919. *Photos Nottingham Public Library*

62 AT MOUNTAIN COTTAGE *c.* 1918. *Photos lent by Mrs W. E. Hopkin*
LAWRENCE AND FRIEDA at Grimsbury Farm, near Newbury *c.* 1911. *Photos lent by Mrs Cecily Lambert Minchin*

63 MAURICE MAGNUS. *Photo lent by H. T. Moore*

64 NORMAN DOUGLAS by Desmond Harmsworth 1933. *By courtesy of Desmond Harmsworth and The University of Texas Library*

65 NORMAN DOUGLAS and Giuseppe Orioli, Austria *c.* 1932. *Photo lent by H. T. Moore*

66 LAWRENCE AND FRIEDA with Pino

Notes

Orioli, Florence c. 1928. *Photo lent by H. T. Moore*

67 PHILIP HESELTINE, the Halliday of *Women in Love*. *Photo lent by H. T. Moore*

68 MRS BORIS DE CROUSTCHOFF, Judith Wood and Philip Heseltine. *Photo lent by Boris de Croustchoff*

69 COMPTON MACKENZIE in 1912, a few years before he first met Lawrence in England. *Photo Radio Times Hulton Picture Library*

71 THE BAY OF TAORMINA, Sicily. *Photo Thames and Hudson Archives*

72 VILLA FONTANA VECCHIA, Taormina, the Lawrences' residence 1920-22. *Photo Derek Patmore*

73 A PORTRAIT of Lawrence by Jan Juta 1920. 15¼ x 11¾ in. Purchased by National Portrait Gallery, London, in 1957. *Photo Peter A. Juley & Son*

74 VILLA BECKER, Val Salice, Turin, where Lawrence stayed briefly with Sir Walter Becker in 1919. In *Aaron's Rod* the villa is transposed to Novara. *Photo lent by H. T. Moore*

75 DOROTHY YORKE, Paris 1917. She was the 'Arabella' of the Lawrence circle. Lawrence portrayed her as Josephine Ford in *Aaron's Rod*. *Photo lent by H. T. Moore*

76 THE BREWSTER FAMILY at Villa Torricella, Capri. Harwood is wearing one of the hair-bands given by 'Uncle David'. *By courtesy of Mrs Harwood Picard*

77 KANDY LAKE and the Temple of the Sacred Tooth, relic of the Buddha. The Lawrences stayed with the Brewsters in the hills above Kandy in 1922. *Photo G. H. Koch*

78 M. L. SKINNER. *Photo lent by Mrs Marjorie Rees*

79 LAWRENCE, Laura Forrester and Frieda at Wyewurk, the Forrester's home in Australia. *Photo A. D. Forrester*
WYEWURK. *Photo F. W. L. Esch*
LAWRENCE, Frieda, the Forresters and other friends on an excursion in 1922. *Photo A. D. Forrester*

80 MABEL DODGE LUHAN. A drawing attributed to Witter Bynner. D. H. Lawrence Collection, The University of Texas.

81 LAWRENCE AND FRIEDA with Indians in New Mexico c. 1923. *Photo lent by H. T. Moore*
MABEL DODGE LUHAN'S former residence at Taos (Lawrence's 'Mabletown'). *Photo Siegfried Mandel*
WILLARD JOHNSON and Witter Bynner with Lawrence at Santa Fe 1923. *Photo lent by Willard Johnson*

82 LAWRENCE'S HOUSE at 4 Zaragoza, Chapala, Mexico 1923. *Photo R. MacNicol*

83 D. H. LAWRENCE c. 1920. *Photo Radio Times Hulton Picture Library*

84 VIEW FROM KIOWA RANCH. *Photo lent by H. T. Moore*

85 LAWRENCE AT KIOWA by Kai Götzsche. D. H. Lawrence Collection, The University of Texas.

86 HOTEL MONTE CARLO. *Photo Joan Carter*
LAWRENCE standing by the mast of the Esmeralda. *Photo Witter Bynner*
ABOARD THE ESMERALDA. The centre group includes Dr George E. Purnell,

Notes

Witter Bynner, Willard Johnson, Idella Purnell Stone, Frieda Lawrence and D. H. Lawrence. *Photo lent by Willard Johnson*

87 THE PYRAMIDS at Teotihucán, Mexico, which the Lawrences visited. *Photo Thames and Hudson Archives*

88 LAWRENCE in 1923. *By courtesy of Professor Majl Ewing*

89 VIEW FROM KIOWA RANCH. *Photo Warren Roberts*

90 LAWRENCE drawn by Knud Merrild *c.* 1923. *D. H. Lawrence Collection, The University of Texas.*

91 THE HON. DOROTHY BRETT in Mexico. *Photo lent by the Hon. Dorothy Brett*

92 LAWRENCE by Dorothy Brett. *D. H. Lawrence Collection, The University of Texas.*

93 KIOWA RANCH in the Sangre de Cristo mountains. *Photo lent by H. T. Moore*
THE KITCHEN at Kiowa. *Photo D. H. Lawrence Collection, The University of Texas*
LAWRENCE with Susan, his cow. *Photo lent by H. T. Moore*

94 INNER CHAMBER in Palace II, Mitla, Oaxaca. *Photo Thames and Hudson Archives*

95 MRS G. R. CONWAY, Lawrence and Frieda in Mexico City, 1925. *Photo D. H. Lawrence Collection, The University of Texas*
LAWRENCE examining pottery. *Photo D. H. Lawrence Collection, The University of Texas*
LAWRENCE talking to a Mexican Indian. *Photo lent by H. T. Moore*
LAWRENCE AND FRIEDA at a market. *Photo D. H. Lawrence Collection, The University of Texas*

LAWRENCE AND FRIEDA with Father Richards. *Photo lent by H. T. Moore*

96 VILLA BERNARDA, Angelo Ravagli's house at Spotorno, which the Lawrences rented 1925-6. *Photo lent by Angelo Ravagli*
D. H. LAWRENCE AND MARTIN SECKER at Spotorno in 1925. *Photo D. H. Lawrence Collection, The University of Texas*

97 ANGELO RAVAGLI. *Photo lent by Angelo Ravagli*

98 LAWRENCE reading *Lady Chatterley's Lover*, a painting by Collingwood Gee. *Photo lent by H. T. Moore*

99 HOTEL LUCCHESI, Florence. *Photo H. T. Moore*

100 VILLA MIRENDA, where the Lawrences lived 1926-8. Most of *Lady Chatterley's Lover* was written here. *Photo Boyce Eakins*

101 LOOKING TOWARDS VILLA MIRENDA. *Photo H. T. Moore*

102 MAGUEY PLANT and organ cacti. *Photo Merle G. Wachter*

103 D. H. LAWRENCE *Photo lent by H. T. Moore*

104 VILLA MIRENDA. *Photo H. T. Moore*

105 UNDER THIS TREE Lawrence wrote much of *Lady Chatterley's Lover*. *Photo lent by H. T. Moore*

106 VILLA MIRENDA. *Photo lent by H. T. Moore*
LAWRENCE AND FRIEDA in the doorway of Villa Mirenda. *Photo lent by Miss F. Gair Wilkinson*

107 PART OF LAWRENCE'S LETTER to Enid

Notes

Hilton c. 1926. Photo lent by H. T. Moore

109 LAWRENCE AND FRIEDA at Villa Mirenda. Photo lent by Miss F. Gair Wilkinson

110 FRESCO from the Tomb of the Leopards, dating from the first quarter of the 5th century BC. Photo Thames and Hudson Archives

111 ALDOUS HUXLEY. Photo Bassano and Vandyk Studios

112 LES DIABLERETS, Switzerland. Photo Swiss National Tourist Office

113 MARIA HUXLEY. Photo Bassano and Vandyk Studios

114 LAWRENCE AND HIS SISTER EMILY at Gsteig bei Gstaad, 1928. Photo lent by Mrs Margaret Needham
BRIGIT PATMORE AND RICHARD ALDINGTON near St Tropez. Photo Derek Patmore

115 HARRY CROSBY in the library of his house at 19 rue de Lille, Paris, 1928. Photo Caresse Crosby
CARESSE CROSBY photographed by Lawrence at Le Moulin du Soleil, Ermenonville, in 1929. Photo lent by Caresse Crosby

116 LAWRENCE at Le Moulin du Soleil. Photo lent by Caresse Crosby

117 EXHIBITION OF LAWRENCE'S PAINTINGS at the Warren Gallery. Photos lent by Philip Trotter

118 DOROTHY WARREN AND PHILIP TROTTER. Photo lent by Philip Trotter

119 A LETTER Lawrence sent to Harry Crosby. By courtesy of Caresse Crosby

120 LAWRENCE in 1929. Photo Ernesto Guardia

121 'BOCCACCIO STORY'. 28 x 47 in. D. H. Lawrence Collection. The University of Texas. Photo Thames and Hudson Archives
'RED WILLOW TREES'. 26 x 40 in. Collection Saki Karavas. Photo Thames and Hudson Archives

122 VILLA BEAU SOLEIL, Bandol, where Lawrence spent the winter of 1929/30. Photo H. T. Moore

123 A VIEW OF VENCE. Photo French Government Tourist Office

124 AD ASTRA SANATORIUM, to which Lawrence went in February 1930. Photo lent by H. T. Moore

125 A BUST OF LAWRENCE by Jo Davidson. From *Apocalypse* published by Martin Secker Ltd in 1932. Photo Nottingham Public Library

126 VILLA ROBERMOND. Photo H. T. Moore
LAWRENCE'S GRAVE at Vence. Photo lent by H. T. Moore

127 LAWRENCE'S TOMB at Kiowa. Photo Warren Roberts

128 EXTERIOR OF LAWRENCE'S TOMB, showing the cross of Frieda's grave. Photo H. T. Moore
INTERIOR OF LAWRENCE'S TOMB. Photo Warren Roberts
THE LAWRENCE FAMILY GRAVE at Eastwood. Photo Warren Roberts

INDEX

Numbers in italics refer to the illustrations

Aaron's Rod, 60, 74*ff.,* 99
Ad Astra sanatorium, 124, *124*
Aldington, Richard, 60, 65, *114,* 115
Apocalypse, 123
Asquith, Lady Cynthia, 42, *43*
Asquith, the Hon. Herbert, 42

Barber, Sir Thomas, 56, *57*
Bavarian Gentians, 122
Beardsall, George (grandfather), 5, *7*
Beauvale Board School, 8, *9*
Bei Hennef, 29*-*30
Birds, Beasts and Flowers, 74
Boccaccio Story (painting), 120, *121*
Boy in the Bush, The, 78, 90
Breach, The, *12,* 14
Brett, the Hon. Dorothy, 91, *91,* 92, 94
Brewster, Achsah, 76, *76,* 77*-*8, 112
Brewster, Earl, 76, *76,* 77*-*8, 110, 112
Brewster, Harwood, 76, *76,* 77*-*8
Brinsley colliery, 5, *5*
British School, *12, 13,* 18
Brooke, Rupert, 45
Burrows, Louise, 17, 26
Bynner, Witter, *81,* 82, *86, 87*

Capri, 66, 76, 96
Carossa, Hans, 122
Carswell, Catherine (born MacFarlane; Mrs H. P. M. Jackson), 45, *45*
Ceylon, 76*-*8, *77*
Chambers, Jessie (Mrs John R. Wood), 15, 16, 17, *17,* 19, 22, 26, 57
Chapala, *82,* 87
Chapala, Lake, *86,* 87
Corke, Helen, 20*ff., 20,* 26, 32
Crosby, Caresse, 115, *115*
Crosby, Harry, 115, *115*

Davidson, Jo, 124
Davidson Road School, 20, *20*

Dax, Alice, 16
Del Monte ranch, 84
Diablerets, Les, 112, *112*
Doolittle, Hilda (Mrs Richard Aldington), 60, *60*
Douglas, Norman, 63, *64,* 65, *65, 98*
Duckworth Ltd, 22, 50

Eastwood, 5, 6, 10, 14, 17
Elephant, 77
England, My England, 47
English Review, 22, 47
Escaped Cock, The, 113, 115
Etruscan Places, 110, *110*

Fantasia of the Unconscious, 68
Felley Mill, *11, 21, 23*
Felley Mill Farm, *25*
Fiascherino, 44, *44*
Flying Fish, The, 103
Fragment of Stained Glass, A, 10

Garda, Lago di, 33, *33*
Gargnano, 33, *34*
Garnett, David, 31, *35, 36*
Garnett, Edward, 22, *22,* 25
Garsington, 49
Gertler, Mark, 124
Glad Ghosts, 42
Götzsche, Kai, 84*-*5, *89*
Greatham, 47, 49

Haggs Farm, *11,* 14, 15, 16, *16*
Heinemann, William, Ltd, 22
Hennef, 30, *30*
Heseltine, Philip (Peter Warlock), *48,* 67, *67,* 68
Hobson, Harold, 33
Holt, Agnes, 20, 26
Hopkin, William E., *62*
Hueffer, Ford Madox (Ford Madox Ford), 22
Hunt, Violet, 22

141

Index

Huxley, Aldous, 111, *111*, 115, 119, 124
Huxley, Maria, 111, 113, *113*
Hymns in a Man's Life, 8

Icking, 31, *31*
Insouciance, 113

Journey With Genius, 82
Joyce, James, 108

Kangaroo, 59, 63, 78, 99ff.
Karavas, Saki, 119
Kiowa ranch, *84*, *89*, 92, *93*, 94, 124
Koteliansky, S. S., 46
Krenkow, Hannah, 30

Ladybird, The, 42
Lady Chatterley's Lover, 10, 31, 97-8, 103, 104ff., 112
Lady Chatterley's Lover, A Propos of, 108, 123
Lamb Close House, 10, *14*, 56
Lawrence and Brett, A Friendship, 91
Lawrence, Arthur John (father), 5, 7, *7*, 11, 12
Lawrence, Emily (Mrs S. King; sister), 7, 8, *114*
Lawrence, Frieda (born von Richthofen; Mrs Ernest Weekley; Mrs Angelo Ravagli), 26-7, *27*, *28*, 29-31, 32, 33-6, 40, 41, *41*, 42, 44, 45, 59-60, *62*, 63, *66*, 77, 79, 80, *81*, 84, *86*, 89, 90, 91, 94, *95*, 124
Lawrence, George (brother), 7, 8
Lawrence, John (grandfather), 5
Lawrence, Lettice Ada (sister), 7, 8
Lawrence, Lydia (born Beardsall; mother), 5, 7, *7*, 11-13, 17, 22, *22*, 57
Lawrence, William Ernest (brother), 7, 8, 13
Life and Works of D. H. Lawrence, The, 57
Litvinov, Maxim, 44
Look! We Have Come Through!, 31, 33
Lorenzo in Taos, 84
Lost Girl, The, 66, 68
Love Poems, 29, 37
Low, Ivy (later Mrs M. Litvinov), 44
Lowell, Amy, 45
Lucas, Percy, 47
Luhan, Antonio (Tony), 80, 82-3
Luhan, Mrs Mabel (born Ganson; Mrs Carl Evans; Mrs Edwin Dodge; Mrs Maurice Sterne), 57, 80ff., *80*

MacCartney, H. B., 21, 32

Mackenzie, Sir Compton, 66, *69*
Magnus, Maurice, 63, *63*, 65, 72
Mansfield, Katherine (born Kathleen Beauchamp; Mrs J. M. Murry), 40, *40*, 41, *41*, 56, 59, 66, 78
Man Who Loved Islands, The, 66
Marsh, Edward, 42, 45
Memoirs of the Foreign Legion, 65, 66
Merrild, Knud, 84-5, 89
Methuen, Ltd, 50
Mexico City, 85, 87, 94
Meynell, Viola, 46, 47
Mohr, Max, 112
Moorgreen Reservoir, 10, *13*, 14
Mornings in Mexico, 103
Morrell, Lady Ottoline, *48*, 49, 55, 67
Morrell, Philip, 49, 52
Mountain Cottage, 60, *61*
Murry, John Middleton, 40, 41, *41*, 56, 59, *59*, 89

Nottingham High School, 8, *9*
Nottingham University College, 18, *18*

Orioli, Giuseppe ('Pino'), 65, *65*, 66, 97, 98, *98*, 104

Paintings of D. H. Lawrence, The, 116
Pansies, 122
Patmore, Brigit, *114*, 115
Pinorman, 65
Plumed Serpent, The, 87, 94, 99, 100ff., 103
Pornography and Obscenity, 123
Portraits from Memory, 49
Pound, Ezra, 22
Prussian Officer, The, 46
Psychoanalysis and the Unconscious, 68

Rainbow, The, 17, 18, 44, 50ff., *51*, 52, 98, 103
Ravagli, Angelo, 96, *97*
Read, Sir Herbert, 122
Red Willow Trees (painting), 121, *121*
Richthofen, Baron Friedrich von, 26, 29, *29*
Richthofen, Baroness von, 29, *29*
Russell, Bertrand, 49ff.

Savage Pilgrimage, The, 45
Sea and Sardinia, 74
Secker, Martin, 67, *96*
Seltzer, Thomas, 67, 88
Ship of Death The 123

Index

Skinner, M. L. ('Mollie'), 78, *78*, 90
Sons and Lovers, 12, 14, 15, 16, 27, 33, 34, 35, 37*ff.*, *37*, 98
Studies in Classic American Literature, 63

Taormina, 71, 72
Taos, 80, 82, 84, 92
Things, 78, 83
Thirroul, 78
Trespasser, The, 21, 22, 32
Twilight in Italy, 33
Two Blue Birds, 66

Vence, 119, *123*, 124
Villa Beau Soleil, 122, *122*
Villa Bernarda, 96, *96*
Villa Fontana Vecchia, 72, *72*
Villa Igéa, *34*
Villa Mirenda, 97, *100*, *101*, 104, *104*, 106, 109, 111
Villa Robermond (now Aurella), 124, *126*
Villard, Oswald Garrison, 89

Warren, Dorothy, 118, *118*
Warren Gallery, 116, *117*, 118
Weekley, Professor Ernest, 19, 26, *28*
Wells, H. G., 22, 124
White Peacock, The, 10, 19, 22, 23*ff.*, 107
Widowing of Mrs Holroyd, The, 11
Woman Who Rode Away, The, 103
Women in Love, 10, 23, 44, 55*ff.*, 67, 98, 103

Yorke, Dorothy, 60, *62*, 75, 115

Zennor, 55, *56*